Granvi
Prefaces t

KING LEAR

Foreword by
Richard Eyre

NATIONAL

NICK HERN BOOKS

First published in this collected paperback edition in 1993 jointl
Nick Hern Books Limited, 14 Larden Road, London W3 7ST
and the Royal National Theatre, London,
by arrangement with Batsford.

Preface to King Lear. Originally published in 1927

Set in 10/11 Baskerville by Pure Tech Corporation, Pondicherry
(India)
Printed in Australia by
Australian Print Group

A CIP catalogue record for this book is available from the British
Library

ISBN 1 85459 157 6

Shakespeare Alive!

The history of the theatre in England in this century can be told largely through the lives and work of two men: George Bernard Shaw and Harley Granville Barker, a triple-barrelled cadence of names that resonates like the ruffling of the pages of a large book in a silent public library. One was a brilliant polemicist who dealt with certainties and assertions and sometimes, but not often enough, breathed life into his sermons; the other a committed sceptic who started from the premise that the only thing certain about human behaviour was that nothing was certain. Both, however, possessed a passionate certainty about the importance of the theatre and the need to revise its form, its content, and the way that it was managed. Shaw was a playwright, critic and pamphleteer, Barker a playwright, director and actor.

The Voysey Inheritance is, at least in my opinion, Granville Barker's best play: a complex web of family relationships, a fervent but never unambiguous indictment of a world dominated by the mutually dependent obsessions of greed, class, and self-deception. It's also a virtuoso display of stagecraft: the writer showing that as director he can handle twelve speaking characters on stage at one time, and that as actor he can deal with the most ambitious and unexpected modulations of thought and feeling. The 'inheritance' of the Voyseys is a legacy of debt, bad faith, and bitter family dissension. Edward's father has, shortly before his death, revealed that he has been cheating the family firm of solicitors for many years, as his father had for many years before that. Towards the end of the play Edward Voysey, the youngest son, confronts the woman he loves:

EDWARD.   Why wouldn't he own the truth to me about himself?

BEATRICE.   Perhaps he took care not to know it. Would you have understood?

EDWARD.   Perhaps not. But I loved him.

BEATRICE.   That would silence a bench of judges.

Shaw would have used the story to moralise and polemicise. He might have had the son hate the father; he might have had him forgive him; he might have had him indict him as a paradigm of capitalism; he would never have said he loved him.

Everybody needs a father, or, failing that, a father-figure. He may be a teacher, a prophet, a boss, a priest perhaps, a political leader, a friend, or, sometimes, if you are very lucky, the real one. If you can't find a father you must invent him. In some ways, not altogether trivial, Granville Barker is something of a father-figure for me. He's a writer whom I admire more than any twentieth-century English writer before the sixties – Chekhov with an English accent; he's the first modern British director; he's the real founder of the National Theatre and, in his *Prefaces*, he's a man who, alone amongst Shakespearean commentators before Jan Kott, believed in the power of Shakespeare on stage.

There was a myth that Granville Barker was the natural son of Shaw. He was certainly someone whom Shaw could, in his awkward way, cherish and admire, educate and castigate. When Barker fell wildly in love ('in the Italian manner' as Shaw said) with Helen Huntington, an American millionairess, he married her, acquired a hyphen in his surname, moved first to Devon to play the part of a country squire, and then to France to a life of seclusion. Shaw thought that he had buried himself alive and could never reconcile himself to the loss. It was, as his biographer

Hesketh Pearson said: 'The only important matter about which he asked me to be reticent.'

After directing many of Shaw's plays for many years, acting many of his best roles (written by Shaw with Barker in mind), dreaming and planning together the birth of a National Theatre, not to mention writing, directing, and acting in his own plays while managing his own company at the Royal Court, Barker withdrew from the theatre, and for twenty years there was silence between the two men. Only on the occasion of the death of Shaw's wife did they communicate by letters. 'I did not know I could be so moved by anything,' wrote Shaw to him.

Out of this self-exile came one major work, slowly assembled over many years: *The Prefaces to Shakespeare*. With a few exceptions (Auden on *Othello*, Barbara Everett on *Hamlet*, Jan Kott on *The Tempest*) it's the only critical work about Shakespeare that's made any impact on me, apart, that is, from my father's view of Shakespeare, which was brief and brutal: 'It's absolute balls.'

As much as we need a good father, we need a good teacher. Mine, improbably perhaps, was Kingsley Amis. He'd arrived, somewhat diffidently, at Cambridge at the same time as I did. The depth of my ignorance of English literature corresponded almost exactly to his dislike of the theatre. Nevertheless, he made me see Shakespeare with a mind uncontaminated by the views of academics, whom he would never have described as his fellows and whose views he regarded as, well, academic. I would write essays marinated in the opinions of Spurgeon, Wilson Knight, Dover Wilson and a large cast of critical supernumeraries. He would gently, but courteously, cast aside my essay about, say, *Twelfth Night*: 'But what do *you* think of this play? Do you think it's any good?' 'Well ... er ... it's Shakespeare.' 'Yes, but is it any *good*? I mean as a *play*. It says it's a comedy. Fine. But does it have any decent jokes?'

I took this for irreverence, heresy even. Over the years, however, I've come to regard this as good teaching, or, closely allied, good direction. It's asking the right questions, unintimidated by reputation, by tradition, by received opinion, or by critical orthodoxy. This was shocking, but healthy, for a young and impressionable man ripe to become a fundamentalist in matters of literary taste and ready to revere F. R. Leavis as the Ayatollah of 'Cambridge English'. What you have is yourself and the text, only that. That's the lesson of Granville Barker: 'We have the text to guide us, half a dozen stage directions, and that is all. I abide by the text and the demands of the text and beyond that I claim freedom.' I can't imagine a more useful and more enduring dictum.

The Prefaces have a practical aim: 'I want to see Shakespeare made fully effective on the English stage. That is the best sort of help I can lend.' What Granville Barker wrote is a primer for directors and actors working on the plays of Shakespeare. There is lamentably little useful literature about the making of theatre, even though there is an indigestible glut of memoirs and biographies, largely concerned with events that have taken place *after* the curtain has fallen. If I was asked by a visiting Martian to recommend books which would help him, her or it to make theatre in the manner of the European I could only offer four books: Stanislavsky on *The Art of the Stage*, John Willett's *Brecht on Theatre*, Peter Brook's *The Empty Space*, and *The Prefaces to Shakespeare*.

Stanislavsky offers a pseudo-scientific dissection of the art of acting which is, in some respects, like reading Freud on the mechanism of the joke: earnest, well-meaning, but devoid of the indispensable ingredient of its subject matter: humour. Stanislavsky's great contribution was to demand that actors hold the mirror up to nature, that they take their craft as seriously as the writers they served, and to provide some sort of formal discipline within which both aims could be realised.

Brecht provided a manifesto that was a political and aesthetic response to the baroque encrustations of the scenery-laden, star-dominated, archaic boulevard theatre of Germany in the twenties. Although much of what he wrote as theory is an unpalatable mix of political ideology and artistic instruction, it is his theatrical instinct that prevails. He asserts, he insists, he browbeats. He demands that the stage, like society, must be re-examined, reformed, that the audience's habits mustn't be satisfied, they must be changed, but just when he is about to nail his 13 Articles to the church door he drops the voice of the zealot: 'The stage is not a hothouse or a zoological museum full of stuffed animals. It must be peopled with live, three-dimensional self-contradictory people with their passions, unconsidered utterances and actions.' In all art forms, he says, the guardians of orthodoxy will assert that there are eternal and immutable laws that you ignore at your peril, but in the theatre there is only one inflexible rule: 'The proof of the pudding is in the eating.' Brecht teaches us to ask the question: what goes on in a theatre?

Brook takes that question even further: what *is* theatre? It's a philosophical, but eminently practical, question that Brook has been asking for over 30 years and which has taken him to the African desert, a quarry in Iran, and an abandoned music hall in Paris. 'I take an empty space and call it a bare stage. A man walks across this empty space while someone else is watching him, and that is all that is needed for an act of theatre to be engaged.' For all his apparent concern with metaphyics, there is no more practical man of the theatre than Brook.

I was once at a seminar where someone asked him what was the job of the director. 'To get the actors on and off stage,' he said. Like Brecht, like Stanislavsky, like Granville Barker, Brook argues that for the theatre to be expressive it must be, above all, simple and unaffected: a distillation of language, of gesture, of action, of design, where meaning is the essence. The meaning must be felt as much as understood. 'They don't have to understand with their ears,' says Granville Barker, 'just with their guts.'

Brecht did not acknowledge a debt to Granville Barker. Perhaps he was not aware of one, but it seems to me that Barker's Shakespeare productions were the direct antecedents of Brecht's work. He certainly knew enough about English theatre to know that he was on to a good thing adapting *The Beggar's Opera, The Recruiting Officer* and *Coriolanus.* Brecht has been lauded for destroying illusionism; Granville Barker has been unhymned. He aimed at re-establishing the relationship between actor and audience that had existed in Shakespeare's theatre – and this at a time when the prevailing style of Shakespearean production involved *not* stopping short of having live sheep in *As You Like It.* He abolished footlights and the proscenium arch, building out an apron over the orchestra pit which Shaw said 'apparently trebled the spaciousness of the stage. . . . To the imagination it looks as if he had invented a new heaven and a new earth.'

His response to staging Shakespeare was not to look for a synthetic Elizabethanism. 'We shall not save our souls by being Elizabethan.' To recreate the Globe would, he knew, be aesthetic anasthaesia, involving the audience in an insincere conspiracy to pretend that they were willing collaborators in a vain effort to turn the clock back. His answers to staging Shakespeare were similar to Brecht's for *his* plays and, in some senses, to

Chekhov's for his. He wanted scenery not to decorate and be literal, but to be expressive and metaphorical, and at the same time, in apparent contradiction, to be specific and be real, while being minimal and iconographic: the cart in *Mother Courage*, the nursery in *The Cherry Orchard*, the dining table in *The Voysey Inheritance*. 'To create a new hieroglyphic language of scenery. That, in a phrase, is the problem. If the designer finds himself competing with the actors, the sole interpreters Shakespeare has licensed, then it is he that is the intruder and must retire.'

In *The Prefaces* Granville Barker argues for a fluency of staging unbroken by scene changes. Likewise the verse should be spoken fast. 'Be swift, be swift, be not poetical,' he wrote on the dressing-room mirror of Cathleen Nesbitt when she played Perdita. Within the speed, however, detailed reality. *Meaning* above all.

It is the director's task, with the actors, to illuminate the meanings of a play: its vocabulary, its syntax, and its philosophy. The director has to ask what each scene is revealing about the characters and their actions: what story is each scene telling us? In *The Prefaces* Granville Barker exhumes, examines and explains the lost stagecraft of Shakespeare line by line, scene by scene, play by play.

Directing Shakespeare is a matter of understanding the meaning of a scene and staging it in the light of that knowledge. Easier said than done, but it's at the heart of the business of directing any play, and directing Shakespeare is merely directing writ large. Beyond that, as David Mamet has observed, 'choice of actions and adverbs constitute the craft of directing'. Get up from that chair and walk across the room. Slowly.

With Shakespeare as with any other playwright the director's job is to make the play live, now, in the present tense. 'Spontaneous enjoyment is the life of the theatre,' says Granville Barker in his Preface to *Love's Labour's Lost*. To receive a review, as Granville Barker did, headed *SHAKESPEARE ALIVE!* is the most, but should be the least, that a director must hope for.

I regard Granville Barker not only as the first modern English director but as the most influential. Curiously, partly as a result of his early withdrawal from the theatre, partly because his *Prefaces* have been out of print for many years, and partly because of his own self-effacement, he has been unjustly ignored both in the theatre and in the academic world, where the codification of their 'systems' has resulted in the canonisation of Brecht and Stanislavsky. I hope the re-publication of *The Prefaces* will right the balance. Granville Barker himself always thought of them as his permanent legacy to the theatre.

My sense of filial identification is not entirely a professional one. When I directed *The Voysey Inheritance* I wanted a photograph of the author on the poster. A number of people protested that it was the height, or depth, of vanity and self-aggrandisement to put my own photograph on the poster. I was astonished, I was bewildered, but I was not unflattered. I still can't see the resemblance, but it's not through lack of trying.

Two years ago the Royal National Theatre was presented with a wonderful bronze bust of Granville Barker by Katherine Scott (the wife, incidentally, of the Antarctic hero). For a while it sat on the windowsill of my office like a benign household god. Then it was installed on a bracket in the foyer opposite a bust of Olivier, the two men eyeing each other in wary mutual regard. A few months later it was stolen; an act of homage perhaps. I miss him.

Richard Eyre

Introduction

We have still much to learn about Shakespeare the playwright. Strange that it should be so, after three centuries of commentary and performance, but explicable. For the Procrustean methods of a changed theatre deformed the plays, and put the art of them to confusion; and scholars, with this much excuse, have been apt to divorce their Shakespeare from the theatre altogether, to think him a poet whose use of the stage was quite incidental, whose glory had small relation to it, for whose lapses it was to blame.

The Study and the Stage

THIS much is to be said for Garrick and his predecessors and successors in the practice of reshaping Shakespeare's work to the theatre of their time. The essence of it was living drama to them, and they meant to keep it alive for their public. They wanted to avoid whatever would provoke question and so check that spontaneity of response upon which acted drama depends. Garrick saw the plays, with their lack of 'art', through the spectacles of contemporary culture; and the bare Elizabethan stage, if it met his mind's eye at all, doubtless as a barbarous makeshift. Shakespeare was for him a problem; he tackled it, from our point of view, misguidedly and with an overplus of enthusiasm. His was a positive world; too near in time, moreover, as well as too opposed in taste to Shakespeare's to treat it perspectively. The romantic movement might have brought a more concordant outlook. But by then the scholars were off their own way; while the theatre began to think of its Shakespeare from the point of view of the picturesque, and, later, in terms of upholstery. Nineteenth-century drama developed along the lines of realistic illusion, and the staging of Shakespeare was further subdued to this, with inevitably disastrous effect on the speaking of his verse; there was less perversion of text perhaps, but actually more wrenching of the construction of the plays for the convenience of the·stage carpenter. The public appetite for this sort of thing having been gorged, producers then turned to newer—and older—contrivances, leaving 'realism' (so called) to the modern comedy that had fathered it. Amid much vaporous theorizing—but let us humbly own how hard it is not to write nonsense about art, which seems ever pleading to be enjoyed and not written about at all—the surprising discovery had been made that varieties of stagecraft and stage were not historical accidents but artistic obligations, that Greek drama belonged in a Greek theatre, that Elizabethan plays, therefore, would, presumably, do best upon an Elizabethan stage, that there was nothing sacrosanct about scenery, footlights, drop-curtain or any of their belongings. This brings us to the present situation.

There are few enough Greek theatres in which Greek tragedy can be played; few enough people want to see it, and they will applaud it encouragingly however it is done. Some acknowledgement is due to the altruism of the doers! Shakespeare is another matter. The English theatre, doubtful of its destiny, of necessity venal, opening its doors to all comers, seems yet, as by some instinct, to seek renewal of strength in him. An actor, unless success has made him cynical, or his talent be merely trivial, may take some pride in the hall mark of Shakespearean achievement. So may a manager if he thinks he can afford it. The public (or their spokesmen) seem to consider Shakespeare and his genius a sort of national property, which, truly, they do nothing to conserve, but in which they have moral rights not lightly to be flouted. The production of the plays is thus still apt to be marked by a timid respect for 'the usual thing'; their acting is crippled by pseudo-traditions, which are inert because they are not Shakespearean at all. They are the accumulation of two centuries of progressive misconception and distortion of his playwright's art. On the other hand, England has been spared production of Shakespeare according to this or that even more irrelevant theory of presentationalism, symbolism, constructivism or what not. There is the breach in the wall of 'realism', but we have not yet made up our minds to pass through, taking our Shakespeare with us.

Incidentally, we owe the beginning of the breach to Mr William Poel, who, with fanatical courage, when 'realism' was at the tottering height of its triumph in the later revivals of Sir Henry Irving, and the yet more richly upholstered revelations of Sir Herbert Tree, thrust the Elizabethan stage in all its apparent eccentricity upon our unwilling notice.[1] Mr Poel shook complacency. He could not expect to do much more; for he was a logical reformer. He showed us the Elizabethan stage, with Antony and Cleopatra, Troilus and Cressida, in their ruffs and farthingales as for Shakespeare's audiences they lived. Q.E.D. There, however, as far as the popular theatre was concerned, the matter seemed to rest for twenty years or so. But it was just such a demonstration that was needed; anything less drastic and provocative might have been passed over with mild approval.

To get the balance true, let us admit that while Shakespeare was an Elizabethan playwright he was—and now is to us—predominantly something much more. Therefore we had better not too unquestioningly thrust him back within the confines his genius has escaped, nor presume him to have felt the pettier circumstances of his theatre sacrosanct. Nor can we turn Elizabethans as we watch the plays; and every mental effort to do so will subtract from our enjoyment of them. This is the case against the circumstantial reproduction of Shakespeare's staging. But Mr Poel's achievement remains; he cleared for us from Shakespeare's stagecraft the scenic rubbish by which it had been so long encumbered and disguised. And we could now, if we would, make a promising fresh start. For the scholars, on their side, have lately—the scholarly among them—cut clear of the transcendental fog (scenic illusion of another sort) in which their nineteenth-century peers loved to lose themselves, and they too are beginning again at the beginning. A text acquires virtue now by its claim to be a prompt book, and the most comprehensive work of our time upon the Elizabethan stage is an elaborate sorting-out of plays, companies and theatres. On Dr Pollard's treatment of the texts and on the foundations of fact laid by Sir Edmund Chambers a new scholarship is rising, aiming first to see Shakespeare in the theatre for which he wrote. It is a scholarship, therefore, by which the theatre of today can profit, to which, by its acting of Shakespeare, it could contribute, one would hope. Nor should the scholars disdain the help; for criticism cannot live upon criticism, it needs refreshment from the living art. Besides, what is all the criticism and scholarship finally for if not to keep Shakespeare alive? And he must always be most alive—even if roughly and rudely alive—in the theatre. Let the scholars force a way in there, if need be. Its fervid atmosphere will do them good; the benefit will be mutual.

These Prefaces are an attempt to profit by this new scholarship and to contribute to it some research into Shakespeare's stagecraft, by examining the plays, one after another, in the light of the interpretation he designed for them, so far this can be deduced; to discover, if possible, the production he would have desired for them, all merely incidental circumstances apart. They might profit more written a generation hence, for the ground they build upon is still far from clear. And this introduction is by no means a conspectus of the subject; that can only come as a sequel. There has been, in this branch of Shakespearean study, too much generalization and far too little analysis of material.[2]

Shakespeare's Stagecraft

SHAKESPEARE'S own career was not a long one. The whole history of the theatre he wrote for does not cover a century. Between Marlowe and Massinger, from the first blaze to the glowing of the embers, it is but fifty years. Yet even while Shakespeare was at work, the stage to which he fitted his plays underwent constant and perhaps radical change. From Burbage's first theatre to the Globe, then to Blackfriars, not to mention excursions to Court and into the great halls—change of audiences and their behaviour, of their taste, development of the art of acting, change of the stage itself and its resources were all involved in the progress, and are all, we may be sure, reflected to some degree in the plays themselves. We guess at the conditions of each sort of stage and theatre, but there is often the teasing question to which of them had a play, as we have it now, been adapted. And of the 'private' theatre, most in vogue for the ten years preceding the printing of the First Folio so far we know least. The dating of texts and their ascription to the usages of a particular theatre may often be a searchlight upon their stagecraft. Here is much work for the new scholarship.

Conversely, the watchful working-out of the plays in action upon this stage or that would be of use to the scholars, who otherwise must reconstruct their theatre and gloss their texts as in a vacuum. The play was once fitted to the stage; it is by no means impossible to rebuild that stage now, with its doors, balconies, curtains and machines, by measuring the needs of the play. It is idle, for instance, to imagine scenes upon inner or upper stage without evidence that they will be audible or visible there; and editing is still vitiated by lack of this simple knowledge. Here, if nowhere else, this present research must fall short, for its method should rightly be experimental; more than one mind should be at work on it, moreover.

The text of a play is a score waiting performance, and the performance and its preparation are, almost from the beginning, a work of collaboration. A producer may direct the preparation, certainly. But if he only knows how to give orders, he has mistaken his vocation; he had better be a drill-sergeant. He might talk to his company when they all met together for the first time to study *Love's Labour's Lost*, *Julius Cæsar* or *King Lear*, on some such lines as these Prefaces pursue, giving a considered opinion of the play, drawing a picture of it in action, providing, in fact, a hypothesis which mutual study would prove—and might partly disprove. No sort of study of a play can better the preparation of its performance if this is rightly done. The matured art of the playwright lies in giving life to characters in action, and the secret of it in giving each character a due chance in the battle, the action of a play becoming literally the fighting of a battle of character. So the greater the playwright, the wider and deeper his sympathies, the more genuine this opposition will be and the less easily will a single mind grasp it, as it must be grasped, in the fullness of its emotion. The dialogue of a play runs—and often intricately—upon lines of reason, but it is charged besides with an emotion which speech releases, yet only releases fully when the speaker is—as an actor is—identified with the character. There is further the incidental action, implicit in the dialogue, which springs to life only when a scene is in being. A play, in fact, as we find it written, is a magic spell; and even the magician cannot always foresee the full effect of it.

Not every play, it must be owned, will respond to such intensive study. Many, ambitiously conceived, would collapse under the strain. Many are mere occasions for display of their actors' wit or eloquence, good looks or nice behaviour, and meant to be no more; and if they are skilfully contrived the parts fit together and the whole machine should go like clockwork. Nor, in fact, are even the greatest plays often so studied. There is hardly a theatre in the world where masterpiece and trumpery alike are not rushed through rehearsals to an arbitrarily effective performance, little more learned of them than the words, gaps in the understanding of them filled up with 'business'—effect without cause, the demand for this being the curse of the theatre as of other arts, as of other things than art. Not to such treatment will the greater plays of Shakespeare yield their secrets. But working upon a stage which reproduced the essential conditions of his, working as students, not as showmen merely, a company of actors might well find many of the riddles of the library answering themselves unasked. And these Prefaces could best be a record of such work, if such work were to be done.

We cannot, on the other hand, begin our research by postulating the principles of the Elizabethan stage. One is tempted to say it had none, was too much a child of nature to bother about such things. Principles were doubtless imposed upon it when it reached respectability, and heads would be bowed to the yoke. Shakespeare's among them? He had served a most practical apprenticeship to his trade. If he did not hold horses at the door, he sat behind the curtains, we may be sure, and held the prompt book on occasion. He acted, he cobbled other men's plays, he could write his own to order. Such a one may stay a journeyman if he is not a genius, but he will not become a doctrinaire. Shakespeare's work shows such principles as the growth of a tree shows. It is not haphazard merely because it is not formal; it is shaped by inner strength. The theatre, as he found it, allowed him and encouraged him to great freedom of development. Because the material resources of a stage are simple, it does not follow that the technique of its playwriting will stay so. Crude work may show up more crudely, when there are none of the fal-lals of illusion to disguise it that the modern theatre provides. But, if he has it in him, a dramatist can, so unfettered, develop the essentials of his art more boldly and more subtly too. The Elizabethan drama made an amazingly quick advance from crudity to an excellence which was often technically most elaborate. The advance and the not less amazing gulf which divides its best from its worst may be ascribed to the simplicity of the machinery it employed. That its decadence was precipitated by the influence of the Masque and the shifting of its centre of interest from the barer public stage to the candle-lit private theatre, where the machinery of the Masque became effective, it would be rash to assert; but the occurrences are suspiciously related. Man and machine (here at any rate is a postulate, if a platitude!) are false allies in the theatre, secretly at odds; and when man gets the worst of it, drama is impoverished; and the struggle, we may add, is perennial. No great drama depends upon pageantry. All great drama tends to concentrate upon character; and, even so, not upon picturing men as they show themselves to the world like figures on a stage—though that is how it must ostensibly show them—but on the hidden man. And the progress of Shakespeare's art from *Love's Labour's Lost* to *Hamlet*, and thereafter with a difference, lies in the simplifying of this paradox and the solving of the problem it presents; and the process involves the developing of a very subtle sort of stagecraft indeed.

For one result we have what we may call a very self-contained drama. Its chief values, as we know, have not changed with the fashions of the theatre. It relies much on the music of the spoken word, and a company of schoolchildren with pleasant voices, and an ear for rhythm, may vociferate through a play to some effect. It is as much to be enjoyed in the reading, if we hear it in imagination as we read, as drama meant to be acted can be. As with its simplicities then, so it should be, we presume, with its complexities. The subtly emotional use of verse and the interplay of motive and character, can these not be appreciated apart from the bare boards of their original setting? It does not follow. It neither follows that the advantages of the Elizabethan stage were wholly negative nor that, with our present knowledge, we can imagine the full effect of a play in action upon it. The imagining of a play in action is, under no circumstances, an easy thing.[3] What would one not give to go backward through the centuries to see the first performance of *Hamlet*, played as Shakespeare had it played![4] In default, if we could but make ourselves read it as if it were a manuscript fresh from its author's hands! There is much to be said for turning one's back on the editors, even, when possible, upon the First Folio with its demarcation of acts and scenes, in favour of the Quartos—Dr Pollard's 'good' Quartos—in their yet greater simplicity.

The Convention of Place

IT is, for instance, hard to discount the impression made merely by reading: *Scene i—Elsinore. A platform before the Castle*; and most of us have, to boot, early memories of painted battlements and tenth-century castles (of ageing Hamlets and their portly mothers for that matter) very difficult to dismiss. No great harm, one protests; it was a help, perhaps, to the unimaginative. But it is a first step to the certain misunderstanding of Shakespeare's stagecraft. The 'if, how and when' of the presenting of localities on the Elizabethan stage is, of course, a complex question. Shakespeare himself seems to have followed, consciously, no principles in the matter, nor was his practice very logical, nor at all consistent. It may vary with the play he is writing and the particular stage he is writing for; it will best be studied in relation to each play. We can, however, free ourselves from one general misconception which belongs to our own over-logical standpoint. When we learn with a shock of surprise—having begun in the schoolroom upon the Shakespeare of the editors, it comes as belated news to us—that neither battlements, throne rooms nor picturesque churchyards were to be seen at the Globe, and that *Elsinore. A platform before the Castle* is not Shakespeare at all, we yet imagine ourselves among the audience there busily conjuring these things up before the eye of faith. The Elizabethan audience was at no such pains. Nor was this their alternative to seeing the actors undisguisedly concerned with the doors, curtains and balconies which, by the play's requirements, should have been anything but what they were. As we, when a play has no hold on us, may fall to thinking about the scenery, so to a Globe audience, unmoved, the stage might be an obvious bare stage. But are we conscious of the scenery behind the actor when the play really moves us? If we are, there is something very wrong with the scenery, which should know its place as a background. The audience was not conscious of curtain and balcony when Burbage played Hamlet to them. They were conscious of Hamlet. That conventional background faded as does our painted illusion, and they certainly did not deliberately conjure up in its place mental pictures of Elsinore. The genus audience is passive, if expectant, imaginatively lazy till roused, never, one may be sure, at pains to make any effort that is generally unnecessary to enjoyment.

With Shakespeare the locality of a scene has dramatic importance, or it has none; and this is as true of his early plays as his late ones. Both in *Richard II* and *Antony and Cleopatra*, scene after scene passes with no exact indication of where we may be. With *Cleopatra* we are surely in Egypt, with Cæsar in Rome. Pompey appears, and the talk tells us that both Egypt and Rome are elsewhere; but positively where Pompey is at the moment we never learn.[5] Indoors or outdoors? The action of the scene or the clothing of the characters will tell us this if we need to know. But, suddenly transported to the Parthian war, our whereabouts is made amply plain. It is, however, made plain by allusion. The information peeps out through talk of kindred things; we are hardly aware we are being told, and, again, we learn no more than we need to learn. This, truly, is a striking development from the plump and plain

> Barkloughly Castle call they this at hand?

of Richard II, even from the more descriptive

> I am a stranger here in Gloucestershire:
> These high wild hills and rough, uneven ways
> Draw out our miles. . .

by which Shakespeare pictures and localizes the manoeuvres of Richard and Bolingbroke when he wants to.
But the purpose is the same, and the method essentially
the same.[6] Towards the end of the later play come scene
after scene of the marching and countermarching of
armies, of fighting, of truce, all the happenings of three
days' battle. Acts III and IV contain twenty-eight scenes
long and short; some of them are very short; three of
them have but four lines apiece. The editors conscien-
tiously ticket them *A plain near Actium, Another part of the
plain, Another part of the plain* and so on, and conclude that
Shakespeare is really going too far and too fast, is indeed
(I quote Sir Edmund Chambers) 'in some danger of
outrunning the apprehensions of his auditory.' Indeed he
might be if this cinematographic view of his intentions
were the right one! But it utterly falsifies them. Show an
audience such a succession of painted scenes—if you
could at the pace required—and they would give attention to nothing else whatever; the drama would pass
unnoticed. Had Shakespeare tried to define the whereabouts of every scene in any but the baldest phrases—the
protesting editors seem not to see that he makes no
attempt to; only *they* do!—he would have had to lengthen
and complicate them; had he written only a labelling
line or two he would still have distracted his audience
from the essential drama. Ignoring whereabouts, letting
it at most transpire when it naturally will, the characters
capture all attention. This is the true gain of the bare
stage; unless to some dramatic end no precious words
need be spent, in complying with the undramatic demands of space and time; incarnation of character can
be all in all. Given such a crisis as this the gain is yet
greater. We are carried through the phases of the three
days' battle; and what other stage convention would
allow us so varied a view of it, could so isolate the true

drama of it? For do we not pass through such a crisis in reality with just that indifference to time and place? These scenes, in their kind, show Shakespeare's stage-craft, not at its most reckless, but at its very best, and exemplify perfectly the freedom he enjoyed that the stage of visual illusion has inevitably lost. His drama is attached solely to its actors and their acting; that, perhaps, puts it in a phrase. They carry place and time with them as they move. The modern theatre still accepts the convention that measures time more or less by a play's convenience; a half-hour stands for an hour or more, and we never question the vagary. It was no more strange to an Elizabethan audience to see a street in Rome turned, in the use made of it, to the Senate House by the drawing of a curtain and the disclosure of Cæsar's state, to find Cleopatra's Monument now on the upper stage because Antony had to be drawn up to it, later on the lower because Cleopatra's death-scene could best be played there; it would seem that they were not too astonished even when Juliet, having taken leave of Romeo on the balcony of her bedroom and watched him descend to the lower stage, the scene continuing, came down, a few lines later, to the lower stage herself, bringing, so to speak, her bedroom with her—since this apparently is what she must have done.[7] For neither Senate House, Monument nor balcony had rights and reality of their own. They existed for the convenience of the actors, whose touch gave them life, a shadowy life at most; neglected, they existed no longer.[8]

Shakespeare's stagecraft concentrates, and inevitably, upon opportunity for the actor. We think now of the plays themselves; their first public knew them by their acting; and the development of the actor's art from the agilities and funniments of the clown, and from round-mouthed rhetoric to imaginative interpreting of character by such standards as Hamlet set up for his players, was a factor in the drama's triumph that we now too often ignore. Shakespeare himself, intent more and more upon plucking out the heart of the human mystery, stimulated his actors to a poignancy and intimacy of emotional expression—still can stimulate them to it—as no other playwright has quite learned to do.

The Speaking of the Verse

His verse was, of course, his chief means to this emotional expression; and when it comes to staging the plays, the speaking of verse must be the foundation of all study. The changes of three hundred years have of themselves put difficulties in our way here; though there are some besides—as one imagines—of Shakespeare's own making. Surely his syntax must now and then have puzzled even his contemporaries. Could they have made much more than we can of Leontes'

> Affection! thy intention stabs the centre;
> Thou dost make possible things not so held,
> Communicat'st with dreams;—How can this be?
> With what's unreal thou coactive art,
> And fellow'st nothing; then, 'tis very credent
> Thou may'st co-join with something; and thou dost;
> And that beyond commission; and I find it,
> And that to the infection of my brains,
> And hardening of my brows.

The confusion of thought and intricacy of language is dramatically justified. Shakespeare is picturing a genuinely jealous man (the sort of man that Othello was *not*) in the grip of a mental epilepsy. We parse the passage and dispute its sense; spoken, as it was meant to be, in a choking torrent of passion, probably a modicum of sense slipped through, and its first hearers did not find it a mere rigmarole. But we are apt to miss even that much. Other passages, of early and late writing, may always have had as much sound as sense to them; but now, to the casual hearer, they will convey more sound than sense by far. Nor do puns mean to us what they meant to the Elizabethans, delighting in their language for its own sake. Juliet's tragic fantasia upon 'Aye' and 'I' sounds all but ridiculous, and one sympathizes with an actress hesitating to venture on it. How far, apart from the shifting of accents and the recolouring of vowels, has not the whole habit of English speech changed in these three hundred years? In the theatre it was slowing down, one fancies, throughout the eighteenth century; and in the nineteenth, as far as Shakespeare was concerned, it grew slower and slower, till on occasions one thought—even hoped—that shortly the actor would stop altogether. There may have been more than one cause; imitation of the French Augustans, the effort to make antiquated phrases understood, the increasing size of the theatres themselves would all contribute to it. The result, in any case, is disastrous. Elizabethan drama was built upon vigour and beauty of speech. The groundlings may often have deserved Shakespeare's strictures, but they would stand in discomfort for an hour or so to be stirred by the sound of verse. Some of the actors no doubt were robustious periwig-pated fellows, but, equally, it was no empty ideal of acting he put into Hamlet's mouth—and Burbage's. We may suppose that at its best the mere speaking of the plays was a very brilliant thing, compared to *bel canto*, or to a pianist's virtuosity. The emotional appeal of our modern music was in it, and it could be tested by ears trained to the rich and delicate fretwork of the music of that day. Most Hamlets—not being playwrights—make a mild joke of telling us they'd as lief the town-crier spoke their lines, but we may hear in it the echo of some of Shakespeare's sorest trials.

The speaking of his verse must be studied, of course, in relation to the verse's own development. The actor must not attack its supple complexities in *Antony and Cleopatra* and *Cymbeline*, the mysterious dynamics of *Macbeth*, the nobilities of *Othello*, its final pastoral simplicities in *A Winter's Tale* and *The Tempest* without preliminary training in the lyricism, the swift brilliance and the masculine clarity of the earlier plays. A modern actor, alas, thinks it simple enough to make his way, splay-footed, through

The cloud-capped towers, the gorgeous palaces . . .

though Berowne's

I, forsooth, in love . . .

or one of Oberon's apostrophes will defeat him utterly. And, without an ear trained to the delicacy of the earlier work, his hearers, for their part, will never know how shamefully he is betraying the superb ease of the later. If we are to make Shakespeare our own again we must all be put to a little trouble about it. We must recapture as far as may be his lost meanings; and the sense of a phrase we *can* recapture, though instinctive emotional response to it may be a loss forever. The tunes that he writes to, the whole great art of his music-making, we can master. Actors can train their ears and tongues and can train our ears to it. We talk of lost arts. No art is ever lost while the means to it survive. Our faculties rust by disuse and by misuse are coarsened, but they quickly recover delight in a beautiful thing. Here, at any rate, is the touchstone by which all interpreting of Shakespeare the playwright must first—and last—be tried.

The Boy-Actress

MORE than one of the conditions of his theatre made this medium of accomplished speech of such worth to him. Boys played the women parts; and what could a boy bring to Juliet, Rosalind or Cleopatra beyond grace of manner and charm of speech? We have been used to women on the stage for two hundred and fifty years or more, and a boy Juliet—if the name on the programme revealed one, for nothing else might—would seem an odd fish to us; no one would risk a squeaking Cleopatra; though, as for Rosalind, through three-parts of the play a boy would have the best of it. But the parts were written for boys; not, therefore, without consideration of how boys could act them most convincingly. Hence, of course, the popularity of the heroine so disguised. The disguise was perfect; the make-believe one degree more complex, certainly, than it needs to be with us; but once you start make-believe it matters little how far you go with it; there is, indeed, some enjoyment in the make-believe itself. But, further, it is Shakespeare's constant care to demand nothing of a boy-actress that might turn to unseemliness or ridicule. He had not much taste for what is called 'domestic drama,' nor does he dose us very heavily with Doll Tearsheet, Mistress Overdone and their like. Constance mourns Arthur's loss, Lady Macduff has her little son, but no mother croons over the child in her arms. Paulina brings Hermione's baby to Leontes, it is true; but see with what tact, from this point of view, the episode is managed. And love-scenes are most carefully contrived. Romeo and Juliet are seldom alone together; never for long, but in the balcony-scene; and in this, the most famous of love-scenes, they are kept from all contact with each other. Consider *Antony and*

Cleopatra. Here is a tragedy of sex without one single scene of sexual appeal. That aspect of Cleopatra is reflected for us in talk about her; mainly by Enobarbus, who is not mealymouthed; but his famed description of her voluptuousness is given us when she has been out of our sight for several scenes. The play opens with her parting from Antony, and in their two short encounters we see her swaying him by wit, malice and with the moods of her mind. Not till the story takes its tragic plunge and sex is drowned in deeper passion are they ever intimately together; till he is brought to her dying there has been occasion for but one embrace. Contrast this with a possible Cleopatra planned to the advantage of the actress of today.

Shakespeare, artist that he was, turned this limitation to account, made loss into a gain.[9] Feminine charm—of which the modern stage makes such capital—was a medium denied him. So his men and women encounter upon a plane where their relation is made rarer and intenser by poetry, or enfranchised in a humour which surpasses more primitive love-making. And thus, perhaps, he was helped to discover that the true stuff of tragedy and of the liveliest comedy lies beyond sensual bounds. His studies of women seem often to be begun from some spiritual paces beyond the point at which a modern dramatist leaves off. Curious that not a little of the praise lavished upon the beauty and truth of them— mainly by women—may be due to their having been written to be played by boys!

Much could be said for the restoring of the celibate stage; but the argument, one fears, would be academic. Here, though, is practical counsel. Let the usurping actress remember that her sex is a liability, not an asset. The dramatist of today may refuse to exploit its allure- ments, but may legitimately allow for the sympathetic effect of it; though the less he does so, perhaps, the better for his play and the more gratitude the better sort of actress will show him. But Shakespeare makes no such demands, has left no blank spaces for her to fill with her charm. He asks instead for self-forgetful clarity of perception, and for a sensitive, spirited, athletic beauty of speech and conduct, which will leave prettiness and its lures at a loss, and the crudities of more Circean appeal looking very crude indeed.

The Soliloquy

THIS convention of the boy-actress may be said to give a certain remoteness to a play's acting. The soliloquy brings a compensating intimacy, and its use was an important part of Shakespeare's stagecraft. Its recognized usefulness was for the disclosing of the plot, but he soon improved upon this. Soliloquy becomes the means by which he brings us not only to a knowledge of the more secret thoughts of his characters, but into the closest emotional touch with them too. Here the platform stage helped him, as the stage of scenic illusion now defeats his purpose. But it is not altogether a question of 'realism' and the supposed obligation this lays upon a real man in a real-looking room to do nothing he would not do if the whole affair were real.

There is no escape from convention in the theatre, and all conventions can be made acceptable, though they cannot all be used indiscriminately, for they are founded in the physical conditions of the stage of their origin and are often interdependent one with another. Together they form a code, and they are as a treaty made with the audience. No article of it is to be abrogated unless we can be persuaded to consent, and upon its basis we surrender our imaginations to the playwright.

With the soliloquy upon the platform stage it is a case—as so often where convention is concerned—of extremes meeting. There is no illusion, so there is every illusion. Nothing very strange about this man, not even the dress he wears, leaning forward a little we could touch him; we are as intimate and familiar with him as it is possible to be. We agree to call him 'Hamlet', to suppose that he is where he says he is, we admit that he thinks aloud and in blank verse too. It is possible that the more we are asked to imagine the easier we find it to do. It is certain that, once our imagination is working, visual illusion will count for little in the stimulating of emotion beside this intimacy that allows the magnetism of personality full play.

There is no more important task for the producer of Shakespeare than to restore to the soliloquy its rightful place in a play's economy, and in particular to regain for it full emotional effect. We now accept the convention frigidly, the actor manoeuvres with it timidly. Banished behind footlights into that other world of illusion, the solitary self-communing figure rouses our curiosity at best. Yet further adapted to the self-contained methods of modern acting, the soliloquy has quite inevitably become a slack link in the play's action, when it should be a recurring reinforcement to its strength. Shakespeare never pinned so many dramatic fortunes to a merely utilitarian device. Time and again he may be feeling his way through a scene for a grip on his audience, and it is the soliloquy ending it that will give him—and his actor—the stranglehold. When he wishes to quicken the pulse of the action, to screw up its tension in a second or so, the soliloquy serves him well. For a parallel to its full effec-tiveness on Shakespeare's stage we should really look to the modern music-hall comedian getting on terms with his audience. We may measure the response to Burbage's

O, that this too too solid flesh would melt . . .

by recalling—those of us that happily can—Dan Leno
as a washerwoman, confiding domestic troubles to a
theatre full of friends, and taken unhindered to their
hearts. The problem is not really a difficult one. If we
solve the physical side of it by restoring, in essentials,
the relation between actor and audience that the intimacy of the platform stage provided, the rest should soon
solve itself.

Costume

THE problem of costume, when it arises, is a subtler one;
nor probably is it capable of any logical solution. Half
the plays can be quite appropriately dressed in the
costume of Shakespeare's own time. It is a false logic
which suggests that to match their first staging we should
dress them in the costume of ours. For with costume
goes custom and manners—or the lack of them. It may
be both a purge and a tonic to the sluggish-fancied
spectator to be shown a Prince of Denmark in coat and
trousers and a Grave-digger in a bowler hat, for reminder that here is a play, not a collection of ritualized
quotations. But physic is for the sick; also, there may be
less drastic cures. When archaeology took hold upon the
nineteenth-century mind it became a matter of moment
to lodge Hamlet in historic surroundings; and withers
were wrung by the anachronisms of ducats and a murder
of Gonzago, French rapiers and the rest. A needlessly
teasing difficulty; why reproduce it in terms of a young
man in a dinner jacket searching for a sword—a thing
not likely to be lying about in his modern mother's sitting
room—with which to kill Polonius, who certainly has
window curtains to hide behind instead of arras? This

gain of intimacy—with a Hamlet we might find sitting opposite at a dinner party—may well be a gain in sympathy. It was originally a great gain, a gift to Shakespeare's audience. But we pay too high a price for it.

What was the actual Elizabethan practice in this matter of costuming is not comprehensively known. We can only say safely that, as with other matters, it was neither constant, consistent, nor, from our present point of view, rational. It was based upon the use of the clothes of the time; but these might be freely and fantastically adapted to suit a particular play or advantage some character in it. Dramatic effect was probably the first consideration and the last. There were such fancy dresses as Oberon or Puck or Caliban might wear; there was always the symbolizing of royalty, and a king would wear a crown whenever he could; there was the utility of knowing Romans from Britons by sight in *Cymbeline*, the martial Roman from the effete Egyptian in *Antony and Cleopatra*, and a Scottish lord when you saw him in *Macbeth*, if we may judge by Malcolm's comment upon Rosse's appearance:

> My countryman; and yet I know him not.

Our difficulty, of course, arises mainly over the historical plays. Not over the English Histories, even so; we can dress Richard III or Henry V by the light of our own superior knowledge of what they wore, and never find it clash violently with anything Shakespeare has put on their backs or in their mouths. But when we come to Julius Cæsar plucking open his doublet, to the conspirators against him with their hats about their ears, and to Cleopatra's

> Cut my lace, Charmian.

not to mention British Imogen in her doublet and hose, we must stop and consider.

The common practice is, in these instances, to ignore the details of Shakespeare's text altogether; to dress Cæsar in his toga, Cleopatra in her habit as she lived, with never a stay-lace about her (though, truly, the costumier, let alone, will tend to get his fashion a few thousand years wrong and turn her out more like the wife of Tutankhamen); and as to Imogen and her surroundings, we do our best to compromise with skins and woad. This may be a lesser evil than presenting a Cæsar recalling Sir Walter Raleigh and a Cleopatra who would make us think of Mary Queen of Scots, but it is no solution of the problem. For the actors have to speak these lines, and if action and appearance contradict them, credibility is destroyed. And the constant credibility of the actor must be a producer's first care. Nor is this all, nor is it, perhaps, the most important thing to consider. The plays are full of reference, direct and indirect, to Elizabethan custom. They are, further, impregnated with what we call 'Renaissance feeling', some more, some less, but all to a degree. Now of this last we have a sense which is likelier to be a better help to their appreciation than any newfangled knowledge of the correct cut of Cleopatra's clothes will be! We know Iago for a Machiavellian figure (so called), and miss none of Shakespeare's intention. But if ever two men breathed the air of a sixteenth-century court, Hamlet and Claudius of Denmark do, and to relate them in habit and behaviour to the twilight figures of Saxo Grammaticus is as much a misinterpretation as any mauling of the text can be. They exist essentially doubtless—as do all the major characters of the plays—in their perennial humanity. But never let us forget the means by which this deeper truth of them is made vivid and actual. There have been better intellects than Shakespeare's, and poetry as good as his. He holds his supreme place by his dramatist's necessary power of bringing thought and vague emotion to the terms of action and convincing speech; further, and far more than is often allowed, by his peculiar gift of bringing into contribution the common-place traffic of life. However wide the spoken word may range, there must be the actor, anchored to the stage. However high, then, with Shakespeare, the thought or emotion may soar, we shall always find the transcendental set in the familiar. He keeps this balance constantly adjusted; and, at his play's greatest moments, when he must make most sure of our response, he will employ the simplest means. The higher arguments of the plays are thus kept always within range, and their rooted humanity blossoms in a fertile upspringing of expressive little things. Neglect or misinterpret these, the inner wealth of Shakespeare will remain, no doubt, and we may mine for it, but we shall have levelled his landscape bare.

Shakespeare's own attitude in this matter of costume and customs was as inconsistent as his practice was casual. He knew what *his* Cæsar or Cleopatra would be wearing and would casually drop in a reference to it. Yet the great Romans themselves were aliens to him. The great idea of Rome fired his imagination. Brutus, Cassius and Antony do not turn typical Elizabethan gentlemen; and to the end of that play he is striving to translate Plutarch. Whenever, on the other hand, even for a moment he has made a character all his own, he cannot but clothe it in lively familiar detail. Cleopatra's are the coquetries of a great lady of his own time, in their phrasing, in the savour. When the heights of the tragedy have to be scaled, manners will not so much matter. But if we make her, at the play's beginning, a pseudo-classic, languishing Oriental, we must do it in spite of Shakespeare, not by his help. What then is the solution of this problem, if the sight of the serpent of old Nile in a farthingale will too dreadfully offend us? We can compromise. Look at Tintoretto's and Paolo Veronese's paintings of 'classic' subjects. We accept them readily enough.

Sometimes, within the boundaries of a play, the centuries seem all at odds. *Cymbeline* need not trouble us, its Roman Britain is pure 'once upon a time'. But in *King Lear*, for instance, Shakespeare is at unwonted pains to throw us back into some heathen past. Yet Edmund is another Iago, Edgar might have been at Wittenberg with Hamlet, and Oswald steps straight from the seventeenth-century London streets. Here, though, the dominant barbarism is the important thing; the setting for Goneril and Regan, Lear's tyranny and madness, and Gloucester's blinding. To a seventeenth-century audience Oswald was so identifiable a figure that it would not matter greatly how he dressed; the modern designer of costume must show him up as best he may. Each play, in fine, if it presents a problem at all, presents its own.

The Integrity of the Text

THE text, one says at first blush, can present no problem at all. The plays should be acted as Shakespeare wrote them—how dispute it? They should be; and it is as well, before we discuss hard cases, to have the principle freely admitted. Lip service enough is done it nowadays, and Colley Cibber's *Richard III*, Tate's *Lear* and Garrick's improvements are at the back of our bookshelves, but we still find Messrs John Doe and Richard Roe slicing out lines by the dozen and even a scene or so, or chopping and changing them to suit their scenery. This will not do. Shakespeare was not a perfect playwright; there can be no such thing. Nor did he aim at a mechanical perfection, but a vitality, and this he achieved. At best then, we cut and carve the body of a play to its peril. It may be robustly, but it may be very delicately organized. And we still know little enough of the laws of its existence, and some of us, perhaps, are not such very skilful surgeons; nor is any surgeon to be recommended who operates for his own convenience.

This good rule laid down, what are the exceptions that go to prove it? There is the pornographic difficulty. This is not such a stumbling block to us as it was to Bowdler, to some bright young eyes nowadays it is quite imperceptible, in fact. Yet, saving their presence, it exists; for it exists aesthetically. Shakespeare's characters often make obscene jokes. The manners of his time permitted it. The public manners of ours still do not. Now the dramatic value of a joke is to be measured by its effect upon an audience, and each is meant to make its own sort of effect. If then, instead of giving them a passing moment's amusement, it makes a thousand people uncomfortable and for the next five minutes very self-conscious, it fails of its true effect. This argument must not be stretched to cover the silliness of turning 'God' into 'Heaven' and of making Othello call Desdemona a 'wanton' (the practice, as I recollect, of the eighteen-nineties), nor to such deodorizing of *Measure for Measure* that it becomes hard to discover what all the fuss is about. If an audience cannot think of Angelo and the Duke, Pompey and Lucio, Isabella and Mistress Overdone, and themselves to boot, as fellow-creatures all, the play is not for them. Othello must call Desdemona a 'whore', and let those that do not like it leave the theatre; what have such queasy minds to do with the pity and terror of her murder and his death? Again, to make Beatrice so mealymouthed that she may not tell us how the devil is to meet her at the gates of hell, 'like an old cuckold with horns on his head', is to dress her in a crinoline, not a farthingale. But suppression of a few of the more scabrous jokes will not leave a play much the poorer; nor, one may add, will the average playgoer be much the wiser or merrier for hearing them, since they are often quite hard to understand.

Topical passages are a similar difficulty. With their savour, if not their very meaning lost, they show like dead wood in the living tree of the dialogue and are better, one would suppose, cut away. But no hard and fast rule will apply. Macbeth's porter's farmer and equivocator will never win spontaneous laughter again. But we cannot away with them, or nothing is left of the porter. Still the baffled low comedian must not, as his wont is, obscure the lines with bibulous antics. There will be that little dead spot in the play, and nothing can be done about it. Rosencrantz' reference to the 'eyrie of children' is meaningless except to the student. Is the play the poorer for the loss of it? But the logic that will take this out had better not rob us of

> Dead shepherd, now I find thy saw of might;
> Who ever loved that loved not at first sight?

And there is the strange case of

The lady of the Strachy married the yeoman of the wardrobe.

Nobody knows what it means, but everybody finds it funny when it is spoken in its place. And this has its parallels.

In general, however, better play the plays as we find them. The blue pencil is a dangerous weapon; and its use grows on a man, for it solves too many little difficulties far too easily.

Lastly, for a golden rule, whether staging or costuming or cutting is in question, and a comprehensive creed, a producer might well pin this on his wall: Gain Shakespeare's effects by Shakespeare's means when you can; for, plainly, this will be the better way. But gain Shakespeare's effects; and it is your business to discern them.

1927

Notes

1 But it should not be forgotten that Sir Herbert Tree, happy in the orthodoxy of public favour, welcomed the heretic Mr Poel more than once to a share in his Shakespeare Festivals.

2 I do not deal in general therefore with certain vexed questions, such as act-division, which still need to be looked at, I think, in the light of the particular play.

3 I remember a most intelligent reader of a modern play missing the whole point of a scene through which the chief character was to sit conspicuously and eloquently silent. He counted only with the written dialogue. I remember, when I thought I knew *King Lear* well enough, being amazed at the effect, all dialogue apart, of the mere meeting, when I saw it, of blind Gloucester and mad Lear.

4 Though, in a sense, there was no first performance of *Hamlet*. And doubtless many of the audience for Shakespeare's new version of the old play only thought he had spoiled a good story of murder and revenge by adding too much talk to it.

5 Unless it may be said that we learn in the scene after whereabouts he *was*.

6 And in *Coriolanus*, which probably postdates *Antony and Cleopatra*, with Marcius' 'A goodly city is this Antium,' we are back to the barely informative. It serves Shakespeare's purpose; he asks no more.

7 I fancy, though, that the later Shakespeare would have thought this a clumsy device.

8 How far this is true of other dramatists than Shakespeare I do not pretend to say; nor how far, with him, the influence of the private theatre, making undoubtedly towards the scenic stage

and (much later) for illusion, did not modify his practice, when he had that stage to consider. A question, again, for the bibliographers and historians.

9   There is no evidence, of course, that he felt it a loss, no such reference to the insufficiency of the boy-actress as there is to the overself-sufficiency of the clown. Women did appear in the Masques, if only to dance, so the gulf to be bridged was not a broad one. But the Elizabethan was as shocked by the notion of women appearing upon the public stage as the Chinese playgoer is today.

King Lear

'LEAR is essentially impossible to be represented on a stage'—and later critics have been mostly of Charles Lamb's opinion. My chief business in this Preface will be to justify, if I can, its title there.

Shakespeare meant it to be acted, and he was a very practical playwright. So that should count for something. Acted it was, and with success enough for it to be presented before the king at Whitehall. (Whatever his faults, James I seems to have had a liking for good drama.) And Burbage's performance of King Lear remained a vivid memory. At the Restoration it was one of the nine plays selected by Davenant for his theatre. He had in mind, doubtless, its 'reforming and making fit'—all of them except *Hamlet* and *Othello* were to suffer heavily from that. But Downes, his prompter, tells us that it was '...*Acted* exactly as Mr *Shakespear* wrote it....'—several times apparently—before Nahum Tate produced his version in 1681. This hotchpotch held the stage for the next hundred and fifty years and more, though from Garrick's time onwards it would generally be somewhat re-Shakespeareanized.[1] One cannot prove Shakespearean stage-worthiness by citing Tate, but how far is it not Tate rather than Shakespeare that Lamb condemns? He has Shakespeare's play in mind, but he had never seen it acted. Part of his complaint is that '... Tate has put his hook in the nostrils of this Leviathan, for Garrick and his followers, the showmen of the scene, to draw the mighty beast about more easily.' And he never considers Shakespeare's play in relation to Shakespeare's stage. He came near to doing so; for, later in the essay, with *The Tempest* for theme, he speaks of '... the elaborate and anxious provision of scenery, which the luxury of the age demands . . .' which '. . . works a quite contrary effect to what is intended. That which in comedy, or plays of familiar life, adds so much to the life of the imitation, in plays which appeal to the higher faculties positively destroys the illusion which it is introduced to aid.' Had he followed out this argument with *King Lear* for an example, giving credit to Shakespeare the playwright as well as to Shakespeare the poet—I do not say that he would have reached a different conclusion, for there is still the plea to be met that here, for once, Shakespeare the playwright did overreach himself, but he must at least have recognized another side to the question. Lamb's essay should be read, of course, as a whole. He loved the drama; the theatre alternately delighted and exasperated him. The orotund acting of his day, its conventional tricks, can have been but a continual offence to his sensitive ear and nicety of taste. He here takes his revenge—and it is an ample one—for many evenings of such suffering. He never stopped to consider whether there might not be more even to the actor's despised art than that.

A profounder and a more searching indictment of the play's stage-worthiness comes from A.C. Bradley in the (for me) most remarkable of those remarkable lectures on Shakespearean Tragedy. To him it seems '. . . Shakespeare's greatest achievement, but . . . *not* his best play.' The entire argument should be read; but this, I think, sums it up not unfairly. He says that 'The stage is the test of strictly dramatic quality, and *King Lear* is too huge for the stage. . . . It has scenes immensely effective in the theatre; three of them—the two between Lear and Goneril and between Lear, Goneril and Regan, and the ineffably beautiful scene in the Fourth Act between Lear and Cordelia—lose in the theatre very little of the spell they have for imagination; and the gradual interweaving of the two plots is almost as masterly as in *Much Ado*. But (not to speak of defects due to mere carelessness) that which makes the *peculiar* greatness of *King Lear*,—the immense scope of the work; the mass and variety of intense experience which it contains; the interpenetration of sublime imagination, piercing pathos, and humour almost as moving as the pathos; the vastness of the convulsion both of nature and of human passion; the vagueness of the scene where the action takes place, and of the movements of the figures which cross this scene; the strange atmosphere, cold and dark, which strikes on us as we enter this scene, enfolding those figures and magnifying their dim outlines like a winter mist; the half-realised suggestions of vast universal powers working in the world of individual fears and passions, all this interferes with dramatic clearness even when the play is read, and in the theatre not only refuses to reveal itself fully through the sense but seems to be almost in contradiction with their reports.' And later: 'The temptation of Othello and the scene of Duncan's murder may lose upon the stage, but they do not lose their *essence*, and they gain as well as lose. The Storm-scenes in *King Lear* gain nothing, and their very *essence* is destroyed.' For this essence is poetry, and, he concludes, '. . . such poetry as cannot be transferred to the space behind the foot-lights, but has its being only in imagination. Here then is Shakespeare at his very greatest, but not the mere dramatist Shakespeare.'

Notice, first of all, how widely Bradley's standpoint is removed from that—we may venture to surmise it—of 'the mere dramatist Shakespeare' and his fellows the actors. To say of certain scenes that they were 'immensely effective in the theatre' and add that they *lost* there 'very little of the spell they have for imagination,' to argue that 'the temptation of Othello and the scene of Duncan's murder may lose upon the stage, but they do not lose their *essence*, and they gain as well as lose'—it would have sounded to them queer commendation. For in whatever Shakespeare wrote was the implied promise that in the theatre it would *gain*. Bradley passes easily to: 'The Storm-scenes in *King Lear* gain nothing, and their very *essence* is destroyed.' But the dramatist, in his defence, would rightly refuse to follow him; for the premises to the argument are not the same.

Bradley and Lamb may be right in their conclusions. It is possible that this most practical and loyal of dramatists did for once—despite himself, driven to it by his unpremeditating genius—break his promise and betray his trust by presenting to his fellows a play, the capital parts of which they simply could not act. Happily for them, they and their audiences never found him out. But if Bradley is right, not the most perfect performance can be a fulfilment, can be aught but a betrayal of *King Lear*. There is the issue. The thing is, of course, incapable of proof. The best that imperfect human actors can give must come short of perfection, and the critic can always retort to their best that his imagination betters it. Bradley's argument is weighty. Yet—with all deference to a great critic—I protest that, as it stands, it is not valid. He is contending that a practical and practiced dramatist has here written a largely impracticable play. Before condemning these 'Storm-scenes' he should surely consider their stagecraft—their mere stagecraft. For may not 'the mere dramatist' have his answer hidden there? But this—starting from his standpoint of imaginative reader—he quite neglects to do.

Ought we, moreover, to assume—as Bradley seems to—that a play must necessarily make all its points and its full effect, point by point, clearly and completely, scene by scene, as the performance goes along? Not every play, I think. For the appreciation of such a work as *King Lear* one might even demand the second or third hearing of the whole, which the alertest critic would need to give to (say) a piece of music of like calibre. But leave that aside. No condoning of an ultimate obscurity is involved. And comedy, it can be admitted, demands an immediate clarity. Nor is the dramatist ever to be dispensed from making his story currently clear and at least provisionally significant. But he has so much more than that to do. He must produce a constant illusion of life. To do this he must, among other things, win us to something of a fellow-feeling with his characters; and even, at the play's critical moments, to identifying their emotions with our own.

Now the *significance* of their emotions may well not be clear to the characters themselves for the moment, their only certainty be of the intensity of the emotions themselves. There are devices enough by which, if the dramatist wishes, this significance can be kept currently clear to the audience. There is the Greek chorus; the earlier Elizabethans turned Prologue and Presenters to account; the *raisonneur* of nineteenth-century comedy has a respectable ancestry. Shakespeare uses the *raisonneur* in varying guises. In this very play we detect him in the Fool, and in Edgar turned Poor Tom. But note that both they and their 'reasoning' are blended not only into the action but into the moral scheme, and are never allowed to lower its emotional temperature by didactics—indeed they stimulate it. For here will be the difficulty in preserving that 'dramatic clearness' which Bradley demands; it would cost—and repeatedly be costing—dramatist and actors their emotional, their illusionary, hold upon their audience. Lear's progress—dramatic and spiritual—lies through a dissipation of egoism; submission to the cruelty of an indifferent Nature, less cruel to him than are his own kin; to ultimate loss of himself in madness. Consider the effect of this—of the battling of storm without and storm within, of the final breaking of that Titan spirit—if Shakespeare merely let us look on, critically observant. From such a standpoint, Lear is an intolerable tyrant, and Regan and Goneril have a case against him. We should not side with them; but our onlooker's sympathy might hardly be warmer than, say, the kindly Albany's.[2] And Shakespeare needs to give us more than sympathy with Lear, and something deeper than understanding. If the verity of his ordeal is really to be brought home to us, we must, in as full a sense as may be, pass through it with him, must make the experience and its overwhelming emotions momentarily our own.

Shakespeare may (it can be argued) have set himself an impossible task; but if he is to succeed it will only be by these means. In this mid-crisis of the play he must never relax his emotional hold on us. And all these things of which Bradley complains, the confusion of pathos, humour and sublime imagination, the vastness of the convulsion, the vagueness of the scene and the movements of the characters, the strange atmosphere and the half-realized suggestions—all this he needs as material for Lear's experience, and ours. Personally, I do not find quite so much vagueness and confusion. To whatever metaphysical heights Lear himself may rise, some character (Kent and Gloucester through the storm and in the hovel, Edgar for the meeting with the blinded Gloucester), some circumstance, or a few salient and explicit phrases will always be found pointing the action on its way. And if we become so at one with Lear in his agony that for the time its full significance escapes us, may not memory still make this clear? For that is very often true of our own emotional experiences. We are in confusion of suffering or joy at the time; only later do we realize, as we say, 'what it all meant to us'. It is, I suggest, this natural bent which Shakespeare turns to his account in these larger passages of *King Lear*. In the acting they move us profoundly. The impression they make remains. And when the play is over they, with the rest of it, should cohere in the memory, and clarify; and the meaning of the whole should be plain. Shakespeare, I protest, has not failed; he has—to the degree of his endeavour—triumphantly succeeded. But to appreciate the success and give effect to it in the play's performance we must master and conform to the stage-craft on which it depends.

In this hardest of tasks—the showing of Lear's agony, his spiritual death and resurrection—we find Shakespeare relying very naturally upon his strongest weapon, which by experiment and practice he has now, indeed, forged to an extraordinary strength, and to a suppleness besides: the weapon of dramatic poetry. He has, truly, few others of any account. In the storm-scenes the shaking of a thunder-sheet will not greatly stir us. A modern playwright might seek help in music—but the music of Shakespeare's day is not of that sort; in impressive scenery—he has none. He has, in compensation, the fluidity of movement which the negative background of his stage allows him. For the rest, he has his actors, their acting and the power of their speech. It is not a mere rhetorical power, nor are the characters lifted from the commonplace simply by being given verse to speak instead of conversational prose. All method of expression apart, they are *poetically conceived*; they exist in those dimensions, in that freedom, and are endowed with that peculiar power. They are dramatic poetry incarnate.

Thus it is that Shakespeare can make such calls upon them as here he must. In the storm-scenes they not only carry forward the story, revealing and developing themselves as they do so, they must—in default of other means—create the storm besides. Not by detachedly describing it; if they 'lose themselves' in its description, they will for that while lose something of their own hold on us. The storm is not in itself, moreover, dramatically important, only in its effect upon Lear. How, then, to give it enough magnificence to impress him, yet keep it from rivalling him? Why, by identifying the storm with him, setting the actor to impersonate both Lear and—reflected in Lear—the storm. That, approximately, is the effect made when—the Fool cowering, drenched and pitiful, at his side—he launches into the tremendous:

> Blow, winds, and crack your cheeks! rage! blow!
> You cataracts and hurricanoes, spout
> Till you have drench'd our steeples, drown'd the cocks!
> You sulphurous and thought-executing fires,
> Vaunt-couriers of oak-cleaving thunder-bolts,
> Singe my white head! And thou, all-shaking thunder,
> Strike flat the thick rotundity of the world!
> Crack nature's moulds, all germens spill at once
> That make ungrateful man.

This is no mere description of a storm, but in music and imaginative suggestion a dramatic creating of the storm itself; and there is Lear—and here are we, if we yield ourselves—in the midst of it, almost a part of it. Yet Lear himself, in his Promethean defiance, still dominates the scene.

But clearly the effect cannot be made by Lamb's 'old man tottering about the stage with a walking-stick'; and by any such competitive machinery for thunder and lightning as Bradley quite needlessly assumes to be an inevitable part of the play's staging it will be largely spoiled. What actor in his senses, however, would attempt to act the scene 'realistically'? (I much doubt if any one of Lamb's detested barnstormers ever did.) And as to the thunder and lightning, Shakespeare uses the modicum to his hand; but it is of no dramatic consequence, and his stagecraft takes no account of it.[3] Yet if the human Lear seems lost for a moment in the symbolic figure, here is the Fool to remind us of him:

> O nuncle, court holy water in a dry house is better than this rain-water out o' door. Good nuncle, in, ask thy daughters' blessing; here's a night pities neither wise men nor fools.

—and to keep the scene in touch with reality. Yet note that the fantasy of the Fool only *mitigates* the contrast, and the spell is held unbroken. It is not till later—when Lear's defiant rage, having painted us the raging of the storm, has subsided—that Kent's sound, most 'realistic' common sense, persuading him to the shelter of the hovel, is admitted.

But Shakespeare has other means of keeping the human and the apocalyptic Lear at one. Though the storm is being painted for us still—

> Rumble thy bellyful! spit, fire! spout, rain!
> Nor rain, wind, thunder, fire are my daughters:
> I tax not you, you elements, with unkindness;
> I never gave you kingdom, call'd you children,
> You owe me no subscription: then let fall
> Your horrible pleasure; here I stand, your slave;
> A poor, infirm, weak and despis'd old man.

—both in the sense of the words and the easier cadence of the verse the human Lear is emerging, and emerges fully upon the sudden simplicity of

> here I stand, your slave;
> A poor, infirm, weak and despis'd old man.

But the actor is not meant, therefore, suddenly to drop from trenchant speech to commonplace, present us a pathological likeness of poverty, infirmity and the rest, divest himself of all poetic power, become, in fact, the old man with a walking-stick. For if he does he will incontinently and quite fatally cease to be the Lear that Shakespeare has, as we said, conceived and embodied in poetry. In poetry; not, one must again insist, necessarily or simply in verse. And it is no more, now or later, a mere question of a method of speaking than of form in the writing. Verse, prose, and doggerel rhyme, in those strenuous scenes, each has its use, each asks an appropriate beauty of treatment, and the three in harmony are, by dramatic title, poetry.

The actor has then, not simply or chiefly to speak poetically, but, for the while, somehow to incarnate this poetry in himself. He can do so—paradoxically—by virtue of an exceptional self-sacrifice. Physically, Shakespeare's Lear must surrender to *him*; he makes himself in return an intellectual and emotional instrument for its expression. That is the way of all honest acting. If the actor's personality is the richer, a character will be absorbed in it. In a play of familiar human commerce actor and character may collaborate, so to say, upon equal terms. But give the character the transcendent quality of poetry, the actor can no longer bring it within the realistic limits of his personality. He may—obtusely—try to decompose it into a realism of impersonation, decorated by 'poetic' speech. It is such a treatment of Lear which produces Lamb's old man with a walking-stick, and, for Bradley, dissipates the poetic atmosphere. But what Shakespeare asks of his actor is to surrender as much of himself as he can—much must remain: all that is physical—to this metaphysical power.

The thing is easier to do than to analyze. Children, set to act Shakespeare, will fling themselves innocently at the greatest of the plays; and, just because they do not comprehend and so cannot subdue the characters to their own likeness, they let us see them—though diminished and feeble—as through a clear glass. For the matured actor it is not quite so easy. He must comprehend the character, identify himself with it, and then— forget himself in it. Yet in this play and these very scenes he will find the example of Lear's own relation to the storm; in the reflection of its grandeur upon him, and the force lent by his fellowship with it to the storm devouring his mind. One must not push the comparison too far, nor is the psychology of acting a subject to be compassed in a sentence or two. But very much as the storm's strength is added to Lear's when he abandons himself to its apprehension, so may the Lear of Shakespeare's poetic and dramatic art be embodied in the actor if he will but do the same. And *there* should be the Lear of Lamb's demand, great 'not in corporal dimension but in intellectual'. Upon a 'realistic' stage the thing cannot well be done. With Shakespeare made to delegate half his privileges to scene-painter and property-man a like dissociation will be forced upon the actor. And it is not only that the apparently real heath and hovel and the all but real thunder and lightning will reduce the characters which move among them to mere matter of fact also, but that by the dissociation itself, the appeal to our imagination—upon which all depends—is compromised. For the strength of this lies in its unity and concentration. It is the unity of the appeal that allows Shakespeare to bring so much within its scope. And, with time, place and circumstance, night, storm and desolation, and man's capacity to match them in despair all caught into a few lines of poetry, it should not be so hard to absorb besides—he willing—the ego of the actor who speaks them. Then he will stand before us not physically ridiculous by comparison with them, but invested with their dynamic quality.

Shakespeare contrives within this harmony the full range of the effects he needs. There are not two Lears—the Titan integrating the storm and the old man breaking under it. In the accommodating realm of dramatic poetry they can remain one. Those contrasted aspects of them are shown in the swift descent we noted from magniloquence to simplicity, from rivalry with the elements to the confession of

> here I stand, your slave;
> A poor, infirm, weak and despis'd old man.

Or, we may say, there are the two Lears in one: the old man pathetic by contrast with the elements, yet terribly great in our immediate sense of his identity with them.

At best, of course, the actor can be but a token of the ideal Lear; and (thanking him) some of us may still feel that in the rarefied spaces of our imagination without his aid we come nearer to Shakespeare's imaginings—though what have we after all but a token of words upon paper to measure these by? But does the actor only remove us a stage further from our source? I think not. He gives the words objectivity and life. Shakespeare has provided for his intervention. He can at least be a true token.

The Main Lines of Construction

King Lear, alone among the great tragedies, adds to its plot a subplot fully developed. And it suffers somewhat under the burden. After a few preliminary lines—Shakespeare had come to prefer this to the grand opening, and in this instance they are made introductory to plot and subplot too—we have a full and almost formal statement of the play's main theme and a show of the characters that are to develop it, followed by a scene which sets out the subplot as fully. The two scenes together form a sort of double dramatic prologue; and they might, by modern custom, count as a first act, for after them falls the only clearly indicated time-division in the play. The Folio, however, adds the quarrel with Goneril before an act-pause is allowed: then—whatever its authority, but according to its usual plan—sets out four more acts, the second allotted to the parallel quarrel with Regan, the third to the climax of the main theme; the fourth we may call a picture of the wreck of both Lear and Gloucester, and in it subplot and main plot are blended, and the fifth act is given to the final and rather complex catastrophe. This division, then, has thus much dramatic validity, and a producer may legitimately choose to abide by it. On the other hand, one may contend, the play's action flows unchecked throughout (but for the one check which does not coincide with the act-division of the Folio). Still it is not to be supposed that a Jacobean audience did, or a modern audience would, sit through a performance without pause. Yet again, it does not follow that the Folio's act-divisions were observed as intervals in which the audience dispersed and by which the continuity of dramatic effect was altogether broken. A producer must, I think, exercise his own judgment. There may be something to be said for more 'breathing-spaces', but I should myself incline to one definite interval only, to fall after Act III. To this point the play is carried by one great impetus of inspiration, and there will be great gain in its acting being as unchecked. If the strain on actors or audience seems to be too great, I should choose a breathing-space after Act I, Scene ii, for all the Folio's authority to the contrary. But the strain should not be excessive upon either audience or actors. Shakespeare's stagecraft—his interweaving of contrasted characters and scenes—provides against this, as does the unity of impression and rapidity of action, which his unlocalized staging makes possible.[4]

The scene in which Lear divides his kingdom is a magnificent statement of a magnificent theme. It has a proper formality, and there is a certain megalithic grandeur about it, Lear dominating it, that we associate with Greek tragedy. Its probabilities are neither here nor there. A dramatist may postulate any situation he has the means to interpret, if he will abide by the logic of it after. The producer should observe and even see stressed the scene's characteristics; Lear's two or three passages of such an eloquence as we rather expect at a play's climax than its opening, the strength of such single lines as

The bow is bent and drawn, make from the shaft

with its hammering monosyllables; and the hard-bitten

Nothing: I have sworn; I am firm.

together with the loosening of the tension in changes to rhymed couplets, and the final drop into prose by that businesslike couple, Goneril and Regan. Then follows, with a lift into lively verse for a start, as a contrast and as the right medium for Edmund's sanguine conceit, the development of the Gloucester theme. Shakespeare does this at his ease, allows himself diversion and time. He has now both the plot of the ungrateful daughters and the subplot of the treacherous son under way.

But the phenomenon for which Shakespeareans learn to look has not yet occurred, that inexplicable 'springing to life'—a springing, it almost seems, into a life of its own—of character or theme. Very soon it does occur; Lear's entrance, disburdened from the care of state, is its natural signal. On his throne, rightly enough, he showed formal and self-contained. Now he springs away; and now the whole play in its relation to him takes on a liveliness and variety; nor will the energy be checked or weakened, or, if checked, only that the next stroke may be intenser, till the climax is past, till his riven and exhausted nature is granted the oblivion of sleep. This is the master-movement of the play, which enshrines the very soul of the play—and in the acting, as I have suggested, there should be no break allowed. To read and give full imaginative value to those fifteen hundred lines at a stretch is certainly exhausting; if they were written at one stretch of inspiration the marvel is that Shakespeare, with his Lear, did not collapse under the strain, yet the exactions of his performance he tempers with all his skill. Lear is surrounded by characters, which each in a different way take a share of the burden from him. Kent, the Fool, and Edgar as Poor Tom are a complement of dramatic strength; and the interweaving of the scenes concerning Oswald, Edmund and Gloucester saves the actor's energy for the scenes of the rejection and the storm.[5]

As the Lear theme expanded under his hand Shakespeare had begun, and perforce, to economize his treatment of the Gloucester-Edgar-Edmund story. Edgar himself is indeed dismissed from the second scene upon no more allowance of speech than

I'm sure on't, not a word.

—with which the best of actors may find it hard to make his presence felt; and at our one view of him before he had been left negative enough. Edmund is then brought rapidly into relation with the main plot, and the blending of main plot and subplot begins.[6] Edgar also is drawn into Lear's orbit; and, for the time, to the complete sacrifice of his own interests in the play. 'Poor Tom' is in effect an embodiment of Lear's frenzy, the disguise no part of Edgar's own development.

As we have seen, while Act III is at the height of its argument, Shakespeare is careful to keep alive the lower-pitched theme of Edmund's treachery, his new turn to the betrayal of his father. He affords it two scenes, of twenty-five lines each, wedged between the three dominant scenes of the storm and Lear's refuge from it. They are sufficient and no more for their own purpose; in their sordidness they stand as valuable contrast to the spiritual exaltation of the others. The supreme moment for Lear himself, the turning point, therefore, of the play's main theme, is reached in the second of the three storm-scenes, when the proud old king kneels humbly and alone in his wretchedness to pray. This is the argument's absolute height; and from now on we may feel (as far as Lear is concerned) the tension relax, through the first grim passage of his madness, slackening still through the fantastic scene of the arraignment of the joint-stools before that queer bench of justices, to the moment of his falling asleep and his conveyance away—his conveyance, we find it to be, out of the main stream of the play's action. Shakespeare then deals the dreadful blow to Gloucester. The very violence and horror of this finds its dramatic justification in the need to match in another sort—since he could not hope to match it in spiritual intensity—the catastrophe to Lear. And now we may imagine him, if we please, stopping to consider where he was. Anticlimax, after this, is all but inevitable. Let the producer take careful note how Shakespeare sets out to avoid the worst dangers of it.[7]

Had the play been written upon the single subject of Lear and his daughters, we should now be in sight of its end. But the wealth of material Shakespeare has posited asks for use, and his own imagination, we may suppose, is still teeming. But by the very nature of the material (save Cordelia) left for development the rest of the play must be pitched in a lower key. Shakespeare marshals the action by which the wheel of Gloucester's weakness and Edmund's treachery is brought full circle with extraordinary skill and even more extraordinary economy. Yet for all this, except in a fine flash or two, the thing stays by comparison pedestrian. He is only on the wing again when Lear and Cordelia are his concern; in the scenes of their reconciliation and of the detached tragedy of Lear's death with the dead Cordelia in his arms, as in the still more detached and—as far as the mere march of the action is concerned—wholly unjustifiable scene of Lear mad and fantastically crowned with wild flowers. We must add, though, to the inspired passages the immediately preceding fantasy of Gloucester's imaginary suicide, an apt offset to the realistic horror of his blinding, and occasion for some inimitable verse. The chief fact to face, then, is that for the rest of the play, the best will be incidental and not a necessary part of the story.[8] The producer therefore must give his own best attention to Albany, Goneril and Regan and their close-packed contests, and to the nice means by which Edgar is shaped into a hero; and in general must see that this purposeful disciplined necessary stuff is given fullness and, as far as may be, spontaneity of life in its interpretation. If he will take care of this the marvellous moments will tend to take care of him.

Shakespeare strengthens the action at once with the fresh interest of the Edmund-Goneril-Regan intrigue, daring as it is to launch into this with the short time left him for its development and resolving. He is, indeed, driven to heroic compressions, to implications, effects by 'business', action 'off', almost to 'love-making by reference only'. Goneril's first approach to Edmund (or his to her; but we may credit the lady, I think, with the throwing of the handkerchief) is only clearly marked out for the actors by Regan's reference to it five scenes later, when she tells us that at Goneril's

> late being here
> She gave strange œilliads and most speaking looks
> To noble Edmund.

(Regan credits her with what, if we prefer our Shakespeare modernized, we might literally translate into 'giving the glad eye'. But this silent business of the earlier scene is important and must be duly marked if the arrival of the two together and Edmund's turning back to avoid meeting Albany, the 'mild husband', is to have its full effect. For the first and last of their spoken love-making, excellently characteristic as it is, consists of Goneril's

> Our wishes on the way
> May prove effects . . . .
> This trusty servant
> Shall pass between us: ere long you are like to hear,
> If you dare venture in your own behalf,
> A mistress's command. Wear this; spare speech;
> Decline your head: this kiss, if it durst speak,
> Would stretch thy spirits up into the air.
> Conceive, and fare thee well.

and Edmund's ('Spare speech', indeed!)

> Yours in the ranks of death!

—all spoken in Oswald's presence too. It is, of course, not only excellent but sufficient. The regal impudency of the woman, the falsely chivalrous flourish of the man's response—pages of dialogue might not tell us more of their relations; and, of these relations, is there much more that is dramatically worth knowing? The point for the producer is that no jot of such a constricted dramatic opportunity must be missed.

For the whole working-out of this lower issue of the play the same warning stands true; an exact and un-blurred value must be given to each significant thing. The interaction of circumstance and character is close-knit and complex, but it is clear. Keep it clear and it can be made effective to any audience that will listen, and is not distracted from listening. Let us underline this last phrase and now make the warning twofold. In working out a theme so full of incident and of contend-ing characters Shakespeare allows for no distraction of attention at all, certainly not for the breaking of conti-nuity which the constant shifting of realistically localized scenery must involve. The action, moreover, of these later scenes is exceptionally dependent upon to-ings and fro-ings. Given continuity of performance and no more insistence upon whereabouts than the action itself will indicate, the impression produced by the constant busy movement into our sight and out again of purposeful, passionate or distracted figures, is in itself of great dramatic value, and most congruous to the plot and counterplot of the play's ending. The order for Lear's and Cordelia's murder, the quarrel over Edmund's pre-cedence, Albany's sudden self-assertion, Regan's sickness, Edgar's appearance, the fight, his discovery of himself, Goneril's discomfiture, the telling of Kent's secret, Regan's and Goneril's death, the alarm to save Lear and Cordelia—Shakespeare, by the Folio text, gets all this into less than two hundred lines, with a fair amount of rhetoric and incidental narrative besides. He needs no more, though bareness does nearly turn to banality sometimes. But unless we can be held in an unrelaxed grip we may not submit to the spell.

He has kept a technical master-stroke for his ending:

Enter Lear with Cordelia in his arms.

There should be a long, still pause, while Lear passes slowly in with his burden, while they all stand respectful as of old to his majesty. We may have wondered a little that Shakespeare should be content to let Cordelia pass from the play as casually as she seems to in the earlier scene. But this is the last of her, not that. Dumb and dead, she that was never apt of speech—what fitter finish for her could there be? What fitter ending to the history of the two of them, which began for us with Lear on his throne, conscious of all eyes on him, while she shamed and angered him by her silence? The same company are here, or all but the same, and they await his pleasure.[9] Even Regan and Goneril are here to pay him a ghastly homage. But he knows none of them—save for a blurred moment Kent whom he banished—none but Cordelia. And again he reproaches her silence; for

Her voice was ever soft
Gentle and low, an excellent thing in woman.

Then his heart breaks.

The Method of the Dialogue

THE dialogue of *King Lear* is remarkable for its combination of freedom and power. Of the plays that neighbour it, the sustained melodies of *Othello* may give greater dignity. In *Macbeth* there are passages that seem to wield

50

a sort of secret sway. *Antony and Cleopatra* has ease and breadth for its normal virtues as *Coriolanus* has strength; and, thereafter, Shakespeare passes to his last period of varied and delightful ease. But the exact combination of qualities that distinguishes the writing of *King Lear* we do not find again; nor indeed should we look to, since it is the product of the matter and the nature of the play. Shakespeare was in nothing a truer artist than in this, that, having mastered his means of expression, journeyed from the rhymed couplets and fantastic prose of *Love's Labour's Lost* to the perfected verse and balanced prose of *Henry V* and the mature Comedies, he yet fettered himself in no fixed style. He may write carelessly; here and there amid the poetic splendours we find what seem to be claptrap couplets and lines flatter than a pancake. But, his imagination once fired, the idea seldom fails of the living vesture it needs. This, it may be said, it is any writer's business to discover. But Shakespeare's art lies in the resource, which can give individual expression to a thought or emotion within the bounds, for instance, of a stretch of formal verse if his first need is for the solid strength of this; or, more often, in the moulding of verse and prose into such variety of expressive form that it is a wonder any unity of effect is kept at all—yet it is. It lies in the daring by which, for a scene or two, he may dispense with all unity of form whatever, if his dramatic purpose will so profit. Witness such a seemingly haphazard mixture of verse, prose and snatches of song as we find in the scenes between Lear, Kent, Gloucester, the Fool and Poor Tom. Yet the dramatic vitality of these scenes lies largely in this variety and balance of orchestration; their emotional strain might be intolerable without it. But the root of the matter, of course, is in the imaginative vitality with which he dowers the characters themselves. It is always instructive to watch Shakespeare getting his play with its crew under way, to see him stating his subjects, setting his characters in opposition. Some lead off, fully themselves from the start, some seem to hang on his hands, saying what they have to say in sound conventional phrase, some he may leave all but mute, uncertain yet, it would seem, of his own use for them. Not till the whole organism has gathered strength and abounds in a life of its own is the true mastery to be seen. Even so, in *King Lear* there is more to be accounted for. In no other of the plays, I think, unless it be *Macbeth*, are we so conscious of the force of an emotion overriding, often, a character's self-expression, and of a vision of things to which the action itself is but a foreground. And how this and the rest of the play's individuality is made manifest by the form as well as the substance of the dialogue, by the shaping and colour of its verse and prose, it is, of course, of primary importance for producer and actors to observe. There is no one correct way of speaking Shakespeare's verse and prose, for he had no one way of writing it. One way grew out of another with him. Little of the method of *Romeo and Juliet* will be left in *King Lear*, much of the method of *Hamlet* still may be. But the fresh matter of a play will provoke a fresh manner, and its interpretation must be as freshly approached.

For more reasons and in more directions than one, Shakespeare seeks strength in simplicity in the writing of *King Lear*. The noble conventional speech of its beginning will not serve him long, for this is the language of such an authority as Lear discards. There is needed an expression of those fiercer, cruder strengths which come into play when a reign of order ends and a moral code is broken. Edmund begins glibly, but is indulged neither with subtle thought nor fine phrases. Goneril becomes like a woman with a fever in her: 'I'll not endure it . . .

I will not speak with him ... the fault of it I'll answer ... I'd have it come to question ... I would breed from hence occasions, and I shall ....' Mark how broken is the eloquence of Lear's appeal to Regan; mark the distraction of his

> No, you unnatural hags,
> I will have such revenges on you both
> That all the world shall—I will do such things,
> What they are yet I know not, but they shall be
> The terrors of the earth. You think I'll weep;
> No, I'll not weep:
> I have full cause of weeping, but this heart
> Shall break into a hundred thousand flaws
> Or ere I'll weep.

Here, one would say, is verse reduced to its very elements.

Shakespeare has, besides, to carry us into strange regions of thought and passion, so he must, at the same time, hold us by familiar things. Lear, betrayed and helpless, at an end of his command of self or circumstance, is dramatically set above the tyranny and logic of both by being made one with the storm, and by his harmonizing with the homely fantasies of the Fool and the mad talk of Poor Tom, till his own 'noble anger' breaks the bounds of reason too. Without some anchorage in simplicity, this action and these characters would range so wide that human interpretation could hardly compass them. Kent does something to keep the play's feet firm on the ground; Gloucester a little; the Fool was to Shakespeare's audience a familiar and sympathetic figure. But Lear himself might escape our closer sympathy were it not for his recurrent coming down from the heights to such moments as

> No, I will be the pattern of all patience;
> I will say nothing.

as

> My wits begin to turn.
> Come on, my boy. How dost, my boy? Art cold?
> I am cold myself. Where is this straw, my fellow?

as

> No, I will weep no more. In such a night
> To shut me out! Pour on, I will endure.
> In such a night as this!

or as

> Make no noise, make no noise; draw the curtains; so, so,
> so. We'll go to supper i' the morning; so, so, so.

This final stroke, moreover, brings us to the simplest physical actualities; Lear's defiance of the elements has flickered down to a mock pulling of the curtains round his bed. Later, when he wanders witless and alone, his speech is broken into oracular fragments of rhapsody; but the play of thought is upon actuality and his hands are at play all the time with actual things; with the flower (is it?) he takes for a coin, with whatever serves for a bit of cheese, for his gauntlet, his hat, for the challenge thrust under Gloucester's blind eyes. Let us note, too, how one of the finest passages of poetry in the play, Edgar's imaginary tale of Dover cliff, consists of the clearest-cut actualities of description. And when Lear wakes to his right senses again, simplicity is added to simplicity in his feeling the pin's prick, in his remembering not his garments. The tragic beauty of his end is made more beautiful by his call for a looking-glass, his catching at the feather to put on Cordelia's lips, the undoing of the button. These things are the necessary balance to the magniloquence of the play's beginning and to the tragic splendour of the storm. Amid the sustained magnificence

of the first scene we find the first use of an even more
simple device, recurrent throughout the play.

> what can you say to draw
> A third more opulent than your sisters? Speak.
> Nothing, my lord.
> Nothing?
> Nothing.
> Nothing will come of nothing; speak again.

Again and again with varying purpose and effect Shakespeare uses this device of reiteration. Note Edmund's

> Why brand they us
> With base? with baseness? bastardy? base, base?
> . . . Well, then,
> Legitimate Edgar, I must have your land.
> Our father's love is to the bastard, Edmund,
> As to the legitimate: Fine word,—legitimate!
> Well, my legitimate, if this letter speed,
> And my invention thrive, Edmund the base
> Shall top the legitimate.

The repetition itself does much to drive in on us the
insistent malice of the man.

Lear summons Oswald with

> O! you sir, you sir, come you hither, sir.
> Who am I, sir?

and the tragic counterpart of this is

> Hear, Nature, hear! dear goddess, hear.

Gloucester's grieved refrain falls casually enough

> O, madam, my old heart is crack'd, is crack'd. . . .
> O, lady, lady, shame would have it hid. . . .
> I know not, madam; 'tis too bad, too bad.

And for a rounded elaboration of the effect, we have Lear's

> O! reason not the need; our basest beggars
> Are in the poorest thing superfluous:
> Allow not nature more than nature needs,
> Man's life is cheap as beast's. Thou art a lady;
> If only to go warm were gorgeous,
> Why, nature needs not what thou gorgeous wear'st,
> Which scarcely keeps thee warm. But, for true need—
> You heavens, give me that patience, patience I need!

Half a dozen other such instances, more or less elaborate, of major and minor importance, can be found; till we come to the effect at its crudest in

> Howl, howl, howl, howl! O, you are men of stones. . . .

and to the daring and magic of

> Thou'lt come no more.
> Never, never, never, never, never!

It is a simple device indeed, but all mature artists tend to seek strength in simplicity of expression. It is, at its simplest, a very old device, and older than drama. Iteration casts, of itself, a spell upon the listener, and the very sound of that echoing 'Never' can make us sharers in Lear's helplessness and despair.[10] Bradley says of this last speech that it leaves us 'on the topmost peaks of poetry'; and so, surely, it does. Rend it from its context, the claim sounds absurd; but dramatic poetry is never to be judged apart from the action it implies.

King Lear—are we still to think?—cannot be acted. The whole scheme and method of its writing is a contrivance for its effective acting. This contrast and reconciliation of grandeur and simplicity, this setting of vision in terms of actuality, this inarticulate passion which breaks now and again into memorable phrases—does not even the seeming failure of expression give us a sense of the helplessness of humanity pitted against higher powers? All the magnificent art of this is directed to one end; the play's acting in a theatre.

The Characters and Their Interplay

LEAR

LEAR himself is so dominant a figure that the exhaustion of his impetus to action with the play's end barely in sight leaves Shakespeare a heavy task in the rallying of its forces for what is still to do. The argument has been raised by then, moreover, to such imaginative heights that any descent from them—even Lear's own—must be precarious. They are heights that Shakespeare himself, perhaps, did not clearly envisage till the soaring had begun. Not that there is anything tentative in the presentation of Lear. Never was character in play, one exclaims, so fully and immediately, so imminently and overwhelmingly set forth! But in this lies the actor's first difficulty.

With the dividing of the kingdom and Cordelia's rejection the trend of the action is clearly foreshadowed:

> So be my grave my peace, as here I give
> Her father's heart from her!

By all the rules of drama we know within a little what the retribution for that must amount to; and Shakespeare will not disappoint us. But equally it would seem that for this massive fortress of pride which calls itself Lear, for any old man indeed of eighty and upwards, there could be no dramatic course but declension. Who would ever think of developing, of expanding, a character from such overwhelming beginnings? Yet this is what Shakespeare does, and finds a transcendent way to do it. So the actor's difficulty is that he must start upon a top note, at what must be pretty well the full physical stretch of his powers, yet have in reserve the means to a greater climax of another sort altogether. It is here, however, that the almost ritual formality of the first scene will help him. The occasion itself, the general subservience to Lear's tyranny (Kent's protest and Cordelia's resolution only emphasize this), Lear's own assertion of kingship as something not far from godhead, all combine to set him so above and apart from the rest that the very isolation will seem strength if the actor takes care to sustain it. There need be, there must be, no descent to petulance. Lear marking the map with his finger might be marking the land itself, so Olympian should he appear. The oath by the sacred radiance of the sun is one that only he may swear. That Kent should call him an 'old man' is in itself a blasphemous outrage.

Come not between the dragon and his wrath. . . .

The bow is' bent and drawn, make from the shaft. . . .

Nothing: I have sworn; I am firm.

Lines like these mark the level of Lear, though their fatality may be a trifle mitigated by the human surliness of

Better thou
Had'st not been born than not to have pleased me better.

by the grim humour which lies in

Nothing will come of nothing: speak again.

in the ironic last fling at Kent of

Away! By Jupiter,
This shall not be revoked.

and in the bitter gibe to Burgundy:

> When she was dear to us we did hold her so,
> But now her price is fall'n. . . .

even, one would like to suspect, in the reason given for his fast intent to shake all cares of state from him, that he may

> Unburden'd crawl toward death.

—for our next sight of his Majesty will show him back from hunting with a most impatient appetite for dinner! Note, too, the hint of another Lear, given us in the music of three short words—the first touch in the play of that peculiar verbal magic Shakespeare could command—when, sated with Goneril's and Regan's flattery, he turns to his Cordelia with

> Now, our joy . . .

But Lear must leave this first scene as he entered it, more a magnificent portent than a man.

He has doffed his kingship; free from its trappings, how the native genius of the man begins to show! It flashes on us as might the last outbursts of some near-extinct volcano. He is old and uncertain; but a mighty man, never a mere tyrant divested of power. He has genius, warped and random genius though it may be, and to madness, as will appear, very near allied. And Shakespeare's art lies in showing us this in nothing he does—for what he does now is foolish—but in every trivial thing that he is. All the action of the scene of the return from hunting, all his surroundings are staged to this end. The swift exchanges with the disguised Kent and their culmination:

> Dost thou know me, fellow?
> No, sir, but you have that in your countenance which I

would fain call master.
What's that?
Authority.

—his encounter with the pernickity jack-in-office Oswald, and with the frail, whimsical Fool who mockingly echoes his own passionate whimsies; all this helps set in motion and sets off a new and livelier, a heartier Lear. Not that Shakespeare bates us one jot of the old man's stiff-necked perversities. He no more asks our sympathy on easy terms for him than will Lear yield an inch to Goneril's reasonable requests. A hundred useless knights about the house—even though, from their master's point of view, they were men of choice and rarest parts—must have been a burden. Lear's striking Oswald really was an outrage; after due complaint Goneril would doubtless have reproved his impertinence—for all that she had prompted it! Even with the petted Fool, and in the very midst of the petting, out there snaps

Take heed, sirrah, the whip!

We need look for no tractable virtues in him.

The play's adopted story has its appointed way to go, but here begins the way of Lear's soul's agony and salvation as Shakespeare is to blaze it. The change in him shows first in the dialogue with the attendant knight and the delicate strokes which inform it. The knight, dispatched to bid that mongrel Oswald come back, returns only to report the fellow's round answer that he would not. 'He would not!' flashes Lear at the unbelievable phrase. But when, picking his words—as, if you were not a Kent (and there had been room at best for but one Kent at Court), no doubt you learned to do with Lear—the knight hints hesitatingly at trouble, the quiet response comes:

Thou but remember'st me of mine own conception: I have perceived a most faint neglect of late; which I have rather blamed as mine own jealous curiosity, than as a very pretence and purpose of unkindness: I will look further into't. But where's my fool? I have not seen him this two days.

Since my young lady's going into France, sir, the fool hath much pined away.

No more of that; I have noted it well. Go you, and tell my daughter I would speak with her. Go you, call hither my fool. O! you sir, you sir, come you hither, sir!

—this last to the mongrel Oswald who has appeared again. But Lear—can this be the Lear of the play's first scene?—to be turning his knight's 'great abatement of kindness' to 'a most faint neglect', and blaming, even so, his own jealous curiosity for noting it! But the Fool's grief for Cordelia he has noted well. Lest it echo too loudly in his proud unhappy heart, with a quick turn he brings the old Lear to his rescue, rasps an order here, an order there, and—takes it out of Oswald.

From now on the picturing of him is lifelike, in that it has all the varied, unexpected, indirect and latent eloquence of life. Shakespeare is at his deftest, his medium at its freest and most supple. Let the interpreter be alert too. This Lear is as quick on the uptake as it is his Fool's business to be. An unnatural quickness in an old man, is it, and some sign of a toppling brain? His silences are as pregnant. He listens and finds cheer in the Fool's chatter and song, throws him an answer or so to keep it alive, snarls now and then like an old lion if a sting goes too deep. Yet his thoughts, we can tell, are away. We must visualize this scene fully and accurately; the Fool carolling, his poor heart being heavy with

Cordelia's loss he carols the more; the old king brooding; and Kent ever watchful, with a dog's eyes. Mark the effect of Goneril's appearance before her father, in purposed, sullen muteness; the Fool's speech points it for us, should we be unobservant; then her break into the prepared formality of verse, as this verse will seem, capping the loose prose of the scene and the Fool's rhyming. Mark, too, the cold kingliness of Lear's four words, all his response to her careful address:

> Are you our daughter?

He resorts to irony, the fine mind's weapon, which blunts itself upon the stupid—for Goneril is stupid, and she has stupidity's stubborn strength. But when the storm of Lear's wrath does break, I think she inwardly shakes a little.

> You strike my people, and your disordered rabble
> Make servants of their betters.

sounds like scared bravado. She can wait, though, for the storm to pass; and, for the moment, it does pass in senile self-reproaches. A few more such futile outbursts, she is confident, and the extravagant old tyrant will be spent and tame enough. But, suddenly, the servants are dismissed and she is alone with husband and father. And her father, rigid, transformed, and with slow, calm, dreadful strength, is calling down the gods' worst curse upon her.

> Hear, Nature, hear! dear goddess, hear!
> Suspend thy purpose if thou didst intend
> To make this creature fruitful! ...

The actor who will rail and rant this famous passage may know his own barnstorming business, but he is no interpreter of Shakespeare. The merely superficial effect of its deadlier quiet, lodged between two whirlwinds of Lear's fury, should be obvious. But its dramatic purpose far outpasses that. Not indifferently did Shakespeare make this a pagan play, and deprive its argument of comfortable faith in virtue rewarded, here or hereafter. And it is upon this deliberate invocation of ill that we pass into spiritual darkness. The terror of it moves Albany rather than Goneril, whom, indeed, nothing is ever to move. But as he rouses himself to plead against it Lear is gone.[11]

Now havoc begins in him. We have his raging, distracted return, tears of helpless despair punctuating hysterical threats; later the stamping, muttering impatience of his wait for his horses. We know that he sets out on a long hard ride, dinnerless after his hunting. Later we learn that the journey was wasted; he had to post on to Gloucester's. Did he ride through the night without rest or pause? Shakespeare is hunting both Lear and the play's action hard and using every device to do it.

Yet the next day when he reaches Gloucester's house— this old man past eighty, and physically we should suppose near exhaustion—he is master of himself, is his most regal self again.[12] We are given the scene with Kent awaked in the stocks to show it.

> Ha!
> Makest thou this shame thy pastime?

All the old dignity in this; there follows the brusque familiar give-and-take which true authority never fears to practice with its dependents; then again the majestic

> Resolve me, with all modest haste, which way
> Thou might'st deserve, or they impose, this usage
> Coming from us.

and the iron self-control in which the shameful tale is

heard. When the tale is ended he still stands silent, while the Fool pipes for us an artless mockery (the art of this!) of his bitter and ominous thoughts. Regan too, Regan too! The grief of disillusion has now become physical pain to him,

> O, how this mother swells up toward my heart;
> *Hysterica passio!* down, thou climbing sorrow!

But he masters it.

> Where is this daughter? . . .
> Follow me not; stay here.

And, solitary in his pride, he goes to face and prove the worst.

If the play, with the invocation of the curse upon Goneril, entered an arena of anarchy and darkness, Lear himself is to pass now from personal grievance to the taking upon him, as great natures may, the imagined burden of the whole world's sorrow—and if his nature breaks under it, what wonder! And Shakespeare brings about this transition from malediction to martyrdom with great art, by contrivance direct and indirect, by strokes broad and subtle; nor ever—his art in this at its greatest—does he turn his Lear from a man into an ethical proposition. The thing is achieved—as the whole play is achieved—in terms of humanity, and according to the rubric of drama.

Lear comes back with Gloucester; the well-meaning Gloucester, whose timid tact is the one thing least likely to placate him. He is struggling with himself, with the old tyrannic temper, with his newfound knowledge of himself, with his body's growing weakness. He is like a great oak tree, torn at the roots, blown this way and that. When the half-veiled insolence of Regan's and Cornwall's greeting must, one would think, affront him, a pathetic craving for affection peeps through. When he once more finds refuge in irony, it is to turn the edge of it against himself. But with four quick shocks—his sudden recall of the outrage upon his servant, the sound of a trumpet, the sight of Oswald, the sight of Goneril— he is brought to a stand and to face the realities arrayed against him. This must be made very plain to us. On the one side stand Goneril and Regan and Cornwall in all authority. The perplexed Gloucester hovers a little apart. On the other side is Lear, the Fool at his feet, and his one servant, disarmed, freed but a minute since behind him. Things are at their issue. His worst errors, after all, have partaken of nobility; he has scorned policy. He has given himself, helpless, into these carnal hands. He will abide, then, as nobly the fate he has courted. Note the single touch of utter scorn for the cur Cornwall, who, the moment looking likely, takes credit for those stocks.

> I set him there, sir; but his own disorders
> Deserved much less advancement.
>   You! Did you!

But all consequences he'll abide, even welcome, he'll abjure his curses, run from one ingrate daughter to the other, implore and bargain, till the depth is sounded and he stands at last surrendered, and level in his helplessness and deprivation with the least of his fellow-men.

> GONERIL.   Hear me, my lord,
>   What need you five-and-twenty, ten, or five,
>   To follow in a house where twice so many
>   Have a command to tend you?
> REGAN.   What need one?
> LEAR. O! reason not the need; our basest beggars
>   Are in the poorest thing superfluous:

> Allow not nature more than nature needs,
> Man's life is cheap as beast's. . . .
>> But, for true need—
> You heavens, give me that patience, patience I need!
> You see me here, you gods, a poor old man
> As full of grief as age, wretched in both!

'O! reason not the need . . .'! This abandoning of the struggle and embracing of misfortune is a turning point of the play, a salient moment in the development of Lear's character, and its significance must be marked. He is now at the nadir of his fortunes; the tragic heights are at hand.

It may be thought that by emphasizing so many minor points of stagecraft the great outlines of play and character will be obscured. But while Shakespeare projects greatly, asking from his interpreters a simplicity of response, lending them greatness by virtue of this convention that passes the play's material through the sole crucible of their speech and action, he yet saves them alive, so to speak—not stultified in an attempt to overpass their own powers nor turned to mere mouthpieces of mighty lines—by constant references to the commonplace (we noted more of them in discussing the methods of the dialogue). He invigorates his play's action by keeping its realities upon a battleground where any and every sort of stroke may tell.

Thus there now follows the tense passage in which Goneril, Regan and Cornwall snuff the impending storm and find good reason for ill-doing. What moralists! Regan with her

> O! sir, to wilful men,
> The injuries that they themselves procure
> Must be their schoolmasters.

Cornwall, with his

> Shut up your doors, my lord; 'tis a wild night:
> My Regan counsels well; come out of the storm.

This is surely the very voice—though the tones may be harsh—of respectability and common sense? And what a prelude to the 'high engender'd battles' now imminent! Before battle is joined, however, the note of Kent is interposed to keep the play's story going its more pedestrian way and to steady us against the imaginative turmoil pending. This use of Kent is masterly; and, in the storm-scenes themselves, the contrasting use of the Fool, feeble, fantastic, pathetic, a foil to Lear, a foil to the storm—what more incongruous sight conceivable than such a piece of Court tinsel so drenched and buffeted!—is more than masterly.

But it is upon Lear's own progress that all now centres, upon his passing from that royal defiance of the storm to the welcomed shelter of the hovel. He passes by the road of patience:

> No, I will be the pattern of all patience:
> I will say nothing.

of—be it noted—a thankfulness that he is at last simply

> a man
> More sinn'd against than sinning . . .

to the humility of

> My wits begin to turn.
> Come on, my boy. How dost, my boy? Art cold?
> I am cold myself. Where is this straw, my fellow?
> The art of our necessities is strange
> That can make vile things precious. Come, your hovel. . . .

and, a little later yet, mind and body still further strained

towards breaking point, to the gentle dignity, when Kent
would make way for him—to the more than kingly
dignity of

> Prithee, go in thyself: seek thine own ease.
> This tempest will not give me leave to ponder
> On things would hurt me more. But I'll go in:
> In, boy; go first.[13]

Now comes the crowning touch of all:

> I'll pray, and then I'll sleep.

In the night's bleak exposure he kneels down, like a child
at bedtime, to pray.

> Poor naked wretches, wheresoe'er you are,
> That bide the pelting of this pitiless storm,
> How shall your houseless heads and unfed sides,
> Your loop'd and window'd raggedness, defend you
> From seasons such as these? O, I have ta'en
> Too little care of this! Take physic, pomp;
> Expose thyself to feel what wretches feel,
> That thou mayst shake the superflux to them,
> And show the heavens more just.

To this haven of the spirit has he come, the Lear of
unbridled power and pride. And how many dramatists,
could they have achieved so much, would have been
content to leave him here! Those who like their drama
rounded and trim might approve of such a finish, which
would leave us a play more compassable in performance no doubt. But the wind of a harsher doctrine is
blowing through Shakespeare. Criticism, as we have
seen, is apt to fix upon the episode of the storm as the
height of his attempt and the point of his dramatic
defeat; but it is this storm of the mind here beginning upon which he expends skill and imagination most

recklessly till inspiration has had its will of him; and the drama of desperate vision ensuing it is hard indeed for actors to reduce to the positive medium of their art—without reducing it to ridicule. The three coming scenes of Lear's madness show us Shakespeare's art at its boldest. They pass beyond the needs of the plot, they belong to a larger synthesis.[14] Yet the means they employ are simple enough; of a kind of absolute simplicity, indeed.

The boldest and simplest is the provision of Poor Tom, that living instance of all rejection. Here, under our eyes, is Lear's new vision of himself.

> What! have his daughters brought him to this pass?
> Could'st thou save nothing? Did'st thou give them all?

Side by side stand the noble old man, and the naked, scarce human wretch.

> Is man no more than this? Consider him well. Thou owest the worm no silk, the beast no hide, the sheep no wool, the cat no perfume. Ha! here's three on's are sophisticated; thou art the thing itself; unaccommodated man is no more but such a poor, bare, forked animal as thou art. Off, off, you lendings! Come; unbutton here.

Here is a volume of argument epitomized as only drama can epitomize it, flashed on us by word and action combined. And into this, one might add, has Shakespeare metamorphosed the didactics of those old Moralities which were the infancy of his art.

> What! hath your grace no better company?

gasps poor Gloucester, bewailing at once the King's wrongs and his own, as he offers shelter from the storm. But Lear, calmness itself now, will only pace up and down, arm in arm with this refuse of humanity:

Noble philosopher, your company.

—nor will he seek shelter without him. So they reach the outhouse, all of his own castle that Gloucester dare offer. What a group! Kent, sturdy and thrifty of words; Gloucester, tremulous; the bedraggled and exhausted Fool; and Lear, magnificently courteous and deliberate, keeping close company with his gibbering fellow-man.[15]

They are in shelter. Lear is silent; till the Fool—himself never overfitted, we may suppose, in body or mind for the rough and tumble of the world—rallies, as if to celebrate their safety, to a semblance of his old task. Edgar, for his own safety's sake, must play Poor Tom to the life now. Kent has his eyes on his master, watching him—at what new fantastic trick? The old king is setting two joint-stools side by side; they are Regan and Goneril, and the Fool and the beggar are to pass judgment upon them.

The lunatic mummery of the trial comes near to something we might call pure drama—as one speaks of pure mathematics or pure music—since it cannot be rendered into other terms than its own. Its effect depends upon the combination of the sound and meaning of the words and the sight of it being brought to bear as a whole directly upon our sensibility. The sound of the dialogue matters almost more than its meaning. Poor Tom and the Fool chant antiphonally; Kent's deep and kindly tones tell against the higher, agonized, weakening voice of Lear. But the chief significance is in the show. Where Lear, such a short while since, sat in his majesty, there sit the Fool and the outcast, with Kent whom he banished beside them; and he, witless, musters his failing strength to beg justice upon a joint-stool. Was better justice done, the picture ironically asks, when he presided in majesty and sanity and power?

But what, as far as Lear is concerned, is to follow? You cannot continue the development of a character in terms of lunacy—in darkness, illuminated by whatever brilliant flashes of lightning. Nor can a madman well dominate a play's action. From this moment Lear no longer is a motive force; and the needs of the story—the absolute needs of the character—would be fulfilled if, from this exhausted sleep upon the poor bed in the outhouse, he only woke to find Cordelia at his side. But Shakespeare contrives another scene of madness for him, and one which lifts the play's argument to a yet rarer height. It is delayed; and the sense of redundancy is avoided partly by keeping Lear from the stage altogether for a while, a short scene interposed sufficiently reminding us of him.[16]

His reappearance is preluded—with what consonance!—by the fantastically imaginative episode of Gloucester's fall from the cliff. There also is Edgar, the aura of Poor Tom about him still. Suddenly Lear breaks in upon them.[17] The larger dramatic value of the ensuing scene can hardly be overrated. For in it, in this encounter between mad Lear and blind Gloucester, the sensual man robbed of his eyes, and the despot, the light of his mind put out, Shakespeare's sublimation of the two old stories is consummated. No moral is preached to us. It is presented as it was when king and beggar fraternized in the storm and beggar and Fool were set on the bench of justice, and we are primarily to *feel* the significance. Yet this does not lack interpretation; less explicit than when Lear, still sane, could read the lesson of the storm, clearer than was the commentary on the mock trial. It is Edgar here that sets us an example of sympathetic listening. His asides enforce it, and the last one:

> O! matter and impertinency mixed,
> Reason in madness!

will reproach us if we have not understood. The train of fancies fired by the first sight of Gloucester, with its tragically comic

> Ha! Goneril with a white beard!

(Goneril, disguised, pursuing him still!) asks little gloss.

> They flattered me like a dog. . . . To say 'Ay' and 'No' to
> everything I said! . . . When the rain came to wet me once
> and the wind to make me chatter, when the thunder would
> not peace at my bidding, there I found 'em, there I smelt
> 'em out. Go to, they are not men o' their words; they told
> me I was everything; 'tis a lie, I am not ague-proof.

Gloucester's dutiful

> Is't not the king?

begins to transform him in those mad eyes. And madness sees a Gloucester there that sanity had known and ignored.

> I pardon that man's life: What was thy cause?
> Adultery?
> Thou shalt not die: die for adultery! No:
> The wren goes to't, and the small gilded fly
> Does lecher in my sight.
> Let copulation thrive; for Gloucester's bastard son
> Was kinder to his father than my daughters
> Got 'tween the lawful sheets.

Gloucester knows better; but how protest so to the mere erratic voice? Besides which there is only the kindly stranger-peasant near. A slight unconscious turn of the sightless eyes toward him, a simple gesture—unseen—in response from Edgar, patiently biding his time, will illuminate the irony and the pathos.

Does the mad mind pass logically from this to some uncanny prevision of the ripening of new evil in Regan and Goneril? Had it in its sanity secretly surmised what lay beneath the moral surface of their lives, so ready to emerge?

> Behold yon simpering dame
> Whose face between her forks presageth snow;
> That minces virtue and does shake the head
> To hear of pleasure's name;
> The fitchew, nor the soiled horse, goes to't
> With a more riotous appetite.[18]

But a man—so lunatic logic runs—must free himself from the tyrannies of the flesh if he is to see the world clearly:

> Give me an ounce of civet, good apothecary, to sweeten my imagination.

And then a blind man may see the truth of it, so he tells the ruined Gloucester:

> Look with thine ears: see how yond justice rails upon yond simple thief. Hark in thine ear: change places, and, handy-dandy, which is the justice, which is the thief? Thou hast seen a farmer's dog bark at a beggar? . . . And the creature run from the cur? There thou might'st behold the great image of authority; a dog's obeyed in office.

It is the picture of the mock trial given words. But with a difference! There is no cry now for vengeance on the wicked. For what are we that we should smite them?

> Thou rascal beadle, hold thy bloody hand!
> Why dost thou lash that whore? Strip thine own back;
> That hotly lust'st to use her in that kind
> For which thou whip'st her. The usurer hangs the cozener.
> Through tattered clothes small vices do appear;
> Robes and furr'd gowns hide all. Plate sin with gold,

And the strong lance of justice hurtless breaks;
Arm it in rags, a pigmy's straw doth pierce it.

Shakespeare has led Lear to compassion for sin as well as suffering, has led him mad to where he could not hope to lead him sane—to where sound common sense will hardly let us follow him:

> None does offend, none, I say, none.

To a deep compassion for mankind itself.

> I know thee well enough; thy name is Gloucester;
> Thou must be patient; we came crying hither:
> Thou know'st the first time that we smell the air
> We wawl and cry. I will preach to thee: mark....
> When we are born, we cry that we are come
> To this great stage of fools.

This afterpart of Lear's madness may be redundant, then, to the strict action of the play, but to its larger issues it is most germane. It is perhaps no part of the play that Shakespeare set out to write. The play that he found himself writing would be how much the poorer without it!

The simple perfection of the scene that restores Lear to Cordelia one can leave unsullied by comment. What need of any? Let the producer only note that there is reason in the Folio's stage direction:

> *Enter Lear in a chair carried by servants.*

For when he comes to himself it is to find that he is royally attired and as if seated on his throne again. It is from this throne that he totters to kneel at Cordelia's feet.[19] Note, too, the pain of his response to Kent's

> In your own kingdom, sir.
> Do not abuse me.

74

Finally, Lear must pass from the scene with all the ceremony due to royalty; not mothered—please!—by Cordelia.

Cordelia found again and again lost, what is left for Lear but to die? But for her loss, however, his own death might seem to us an arbitrary stroke; since the old Lear, we may say, is already dead. Shakespeare, moreover, has transported him beyond all worldly issues. This is, perhaps, why the action of the battle which will seemingly defeat his fortunes is minimized. What does defeat matter to him—or even victory? It is certainly the key to the meaning of the scene which follows. Cordelia, who would 'out-frown false fortune's frown', is ready to face her sisters and to shame them—were there a chance of it!—with the sight of her father's wrongs. But Lear himself has no interest in anything of the sort.

> No, no, no, no! Come, let's away to prison.
> We two alone will sing like birds i' the cage:
> When thou dost ask me blessing, I'll kneel down,
> And ask of thee forgiveness[20]: so we'll live,
> And pray, and sing, and tell old tales, and laugh
> At gilded butterflies, and hear poor rogues
> Talk of court news. . . .

He has passed beyond care for revenge or success, beyond even the questioning of rights and wrongs. Better indeed to be oppressed, if so you can be safe from contention. Prison will bring him freedom.

> Upon such sacrifices, my Cordelia,
> The gods themselves throw incense. Have I caught thee?
> He that parts us shall bring a brand from heaven
> And fire us hence like foxes. Wipe thine eyes;
> The good years shall devour them, flesh and fell,
> Ere they shall make us weep: we'll see 'em starve first.

Lear's death, upon one ground or another, is artistically inevitable. Try to imagine his survival; no further argument will be needed. The death of Cordelia has been condemned as a wanton outrage upon our feelings and so as an aesthetic blot upon the play. But the dramatic mind that was working to the tune of

> As flies to wanton boys are we to the gods;
> They kill us for their sport.

was not likely to be swayed by sentiment. The tragic truth about life, to the Shakespeare that wrote *King Lear*, included its capricious cruelty. And what meeter sacrifice to this than Cordelia? Besides, as we have seen, he must provide this new Lear with a tragic determinant, since 'the great rage . . . is kill'd in him', which precipitated catastrophe for the old Lear. And what but Cordelia's loss would suffice?

We have already set Lear's last scene in comparison with his first; it will be worth while to note a little more particularly the likeness and the difference. The same commanding figure; he bears the body of Cordelia as lightly as ever he carried robe, crown and sceptre before. All he has undergone has not so bated his colossal strength but that he could kill her murderer with his bare hands.

> I kill'd the slave that was a-hanging thee.
> Tis true, my lords, he did.

says the officer in answer to their amazed looks. Albany, Edgar, Kent and the rest stand silent and intent around him; Regan and Goneril are there, silent too. He stands, with the limp body close clasped, glaring blankly at them for a moment. When speech is torn from him, in place of the old kingly rhetoric we have only the horrible, half human

Howl, howl, howl, howl!

Who these are, for all their dignity and martial splendour, for all the respect they show him, he neither knows nor cares. They are men of stone and murderous traitors; though, after a little, through the mist of his suffering, comes a word for Kent. All his world, of power and passion and will, and the wider world of thought over which his mind in its ecstasy had ranged, is narrowed now to Cordelia; and she is dead in his arms.

Here is the clue to the scene; this terrible concentration upon the dead, and upon the unconquerable fact of death. This thing was Cordelia; she was alive, she is dead. Here is human tragedy brought to its simplest terms, fit ending to a tragic play that has seemed to outleap human experience. From power of intellect and will, from the imaginative sweep of madness, Shakespeare brings Lear to this; to no moralizing nor high thoughts, but just to

> She's gone for ever.
> I know when one is dead and when one lives;
> She's dead as earth. Lend me a looking-glass;
> If that her breath will mist or stain the stone,
> Why, then she lives.

Lacking a glass, he catches at a floating feather. That stirs on her lips; a last mockery. Kent kneels by him to share his grief. Then to the bystanders comes the news of Edmund's death; the business of life goes forward, as it will, and draws attention from him for a moment. But what does he heed? When they turn back to him he has her broken body in his arms again.

> And my poor fool is hang'd. No, no, no life!
> Why should a dog, a horse, a rat, have life,

And thou no breath at all? Thou'lt come no more,
Never, never, never, never, never!
Pray you, undo this button; thank you, sir.
Do you see this? Look on her, look, her lips,
Look there, look there!²¹

GONERIL, REGAN AND CORDELIA

Shakespeare's point of departure for all three is that of
the crude old story. Moreover, with regard to Goneril
and Regan he is quite content to assume—we shrink
from the assumption nowadays—that there are really
wicked people in the world. That admitted, these two
exemplars of the fact are lifelike enough. Their aspect
may be determined by the story's needs, but their significance does not end here; and, within the limits afforded
them, they develop freely and naturally, each in her own
way.

Likeness and difference are marked from the beginning. They are both realists. Their father wants smooth
speech of them and they give it, echoing his very phrases
and tones. They ignore Cordelia's reproaches; she is
exiled and in disgrace, so they safely may. Left alone
together (and the drop here from verse to prose seems
to bring us with something of a bump to the plain truth
about them), they are under no illusions at all, we find,
about their own good fortune.

> he always loved our sister most; and with what poor
> judgment he hath now cast her off appears too grossly.

There are few things more unlovely than the passionless
appraisement of evil and our profit in it. They are as
wide-awake to the chances of trouble ahead; but while
Regan would wait and see, Goneril means to go to meet
it.

If the quarrel between King Lear and his two daughters had been brought into the law courts, counsels' speeches for Regan and Goneril would have been interesting. But what a good case Goneril makes for herself unaided! The setting-on of Oswald to provoke Lear might, one supposes, have been kept out of the evidence. True, the reservation of a hundred knights was a definite condition of his abdication. But their behaviour was impeachable; it may well have been if Lear's own treatment of Oswald set them an example. He was almost in his dotage; unbalanced certainly. His outbursts of ironic rage, the cursing of Goneril, his subsequent ravings—his whole conduct shows him unfit to look after himself. For his own sake, then, how much better for his daughters' servants to wait on him! And Regan, though she needs Goneril's prompting, makes an even better case of it; the weaker nature is the more plausible. A jury of men and women of common sense might well give their verdict against Lear; and we can hear the judge ruling upon the one point of law in his favour with grave misgiving that he is doing him no good. How then can we call Regan and Goneril double-dyed fiends? They played the hypocrite for a kingdom; but which of us might not? Having got what they wanted and more than they expected they found good excuse for not paying the price for it. Like failings have been known in the most reputable people. Their conduct so far, it could be argued, has been eminently respectable, level-headed and worldly-wise. They do seem somewhat hard-hearted, but that is all. Says the broken, mad old king:

> let them anatomize Regan, see what breeds about her
> heart. Is there any cause in nature that makes these hard
> hearts?

But from now on the truth about them grows patent. Does prosperity turn their heads? It releases hidden devils. When Gloucester's defection is discovered they waste no words.

> Hang him instantly.
> Pluck out his eyes.

And the weaker Regan grows the more violent of the two; she turns crueller even than that bloody wolf, Cornwall, her husband. For amid the scuffling a little later she can think to tell Gloucester that his own son has betrayed him; and even as he faces her, blinded and bleeding, she can jeer at him.

The devil of lust comes now to match with the devil of cruelty. Goneril has hardly seen Edmund but she marks him down with those

> strange œilliads and most speaking looks . . .

—which rouse Regan to jealousy as quickly. In their plot upon their father they were clever enough, self-controlled, subtle. But, the beast let loose in them, they turn reckless, shameless, foolish. Regan, with a little law on her side, presumes on it; so Goneril poisons her as she might a rat. And the last note of Goneril is one of devilish pride.

> Say, if I do, the laws are mine, not thine:
> Who can arraign me for it?

Flinging this at her husband when he confronts her with the proof that she meant to have his life, she departs to take her own.

We may see, then, in Goneril and Regan, evil triumphant, self-degrading and self-destructive. It may also be that, from beginning to end, Shakespeare, for his part, sees little to choose between hot lust and murdering hand and the hard heart, in which all is rooted.

It will be a fatal error to present Cordelia as a meek saint. She has more than a touch of her father in her. She is as proud as he is, and as obstinate, for all her sweetness and her youth. And, being young, she answers uncalculatingly with pride to his pride even as later she answers with pity to his misery. To miss this likeness between the two is to miss Shakespeare's first important dramatic effect; the mighty old man and the frail child, confronted, and each unyielding.

> So young and so untender?
> So young, my lord, and true.

And they both have the right of it, after all. If age owes some tolerance to youth, it may be thought too that youth owes to age and fatherhood something more—and less—than the truth. But she has courage, has Cordelia, amazing courage. Princess though she be, it is no small matter to stand her ground before Lear, throned in the plenitude of his power, to stand up to him without effort, explanation or excuse. Nor does she wince at the penalty, nor to the end utter one pleading word. Nor, be it noted, does Kent, who is of her temper, ask pity for her. His chief concern is to warn Lear against his own folly and its consequences.[22] It is her strength of mind he emphasizes and praises.

> The gods to their dear shelter take thee, maid,
> That justly think'st and hast most rightly said!

Nor would she, apparently, open her mouth again to her father but that she means her character shall be cleared. And even this approach to him is formal and uncompromising:

> I yet beseech your majesty . . .

She does (Shakespeare keeps her human) slip in, as if it

hardly mattered, a dozen words of vindication:

> . . . since what I well intend,
> I'll do't before I speak.

Yet, lest even that should seem weakness, she nullifies its effect for a finish. Nor does Lear respond, nor exonerate her except by a noncommittal growl. Still, she is not hard.

> The jewels of our father, with wash'd eyes
> Cordelia leaves you. . . .

Shakespeare has provided in this encounter between Cordelia and Lear that prime necessity of drama, clash of character; that sharpest clash, moreover, of like in opposition to like. He has added wonder and beauty by setting these twin spirits in noble and contrasted habitations. Pride unchecked in Lear has grown monstrous and diseased with his years. In her youth it shows unspoiled, it is in flower. But it is the same pride.

The technical achievement in Shakespeare's staging of Cordelia is his gain of a maximum effect by a minimum of means. It is a triumph of what may be called 'placing'. The character itself has, to begin with, that vitality which positive virtues give. Cordelia is never in doubt about herself; she has no vagaries, she is what she is all circumstances apart, what she says seems to come new-minted from her mind, and our impression of her is as clean cut. Add to this her calm and steadfast isolation among the contending or subservient figures of that first scene—and the fact, of course, that from this very thrift of herself the broadcast violence of the play's whole action springs—then we see how, with but a reminder of her here and there, Shakespeare could trust to her reappearance after long delay, no jot of her importance nor of our interest in her bated. Indeed, if the Folio text gives us in the main his own reconsiderations, he found his first care to reinstate her in our sympathy a scene before she reappears to be needless.[23] But at this point the play itself is beginning to have need of her return. Somehow its intolerable agonies must be eased; and amid the dreadful flux our memory of her certainty abides.

There is not, at any time, much to explain in Cordelia. Nor does she now herself protest her love and expand her forgiveness. She has not changed; elaboration would only falsify her. Not that she is by nature taciturn; she can resolve the harmonies of her mind, and Shakespeare gives a flowing music to them.

> Was this a face
> To be opposed against the warring winds?
> To stand against the deep dread-bolted thunder?
> In the most terrible and nimble stroke
> Of quick cross lightning? to watch—poor perdu!
> With this thin helm? Mine enemy's dog,
> Though he had bit me, should have stood that night
> Against my fire.

But even this is not spoken to Lear. To him she still says little. It is as if speech itself were not a simple or genuine enough thing for the expressing of her deep heart. And her

> No cause, no cause!

when he would welcome her reproaches, is not at all the kindly, conventional, superior 'Let's forget it' of the morally offended. It is but the complement of that 'Nothing' which cost her a kingdom, and as true of her in its tenderness as the other was true. For the simple secret of Cordelia's nature is that she does not see things from the standpoint of her own gain or loss. She did not beg, she does not bargain. She can give as she could lose, keeping a quiet mind. It is no effort to her to love her father better than herself. Yet this supremest virtue, as we count it, is no gain to him; we must note this too. Her wisdom of heart showed her Regan and Goneril as they were; yet it was an inarticulate wisdom and provoked evil in Lear, and could but hold her bound in patience till the evil was purged. Is there, then, an impotence in such goodness, lovely as we find it? And is this why Shakespeare lets her slip out of the play a few scenes later to her death, as if, for all her beauty of spirit, she were not of so much account? Neither good fortune nor ill can touch Cordelia herself; this is her strength and her weakness both.

> For thee, oppressed king, am I cast down;
> Myself could else outfrown false fortune's frown. . . .

she says; and so she could, we are sure. Then she falls into dumbness—into such a dumbness as was her first undoing—and passes, silent, from our sight.

KENT

Here is another positive, absolute being; he, Lear and Cordelia make a trinity of them. He has not Lear's perilous intellect nor Cordelia's peace of soul. His dominant quality is his unquestioning courage; akin to this the selflessness which makes it as easy for him to be silent as to speak. And he springs from Shakespeare's imagination all complete; full-flavoured and consistent from the first. Surer sign yet of his author's certainty about him is the natural inconsistency of the man as we see him. Through the first three acts there is never a stroke in the drawing of Kent which is merely conventional, nor yet an uncertain one.[24] But neither is there one which, however unexpected, need perplex us. And for a small sign of Shakespeare's confidence in the sufficiency of his creature, see the shrewd critical thrust which he lets Cornwall have at him:

> This is some fellow,
> Who, having been praised for bluntness, doth affect
> A saucy roughness. . . .

Even though it be a Cornwall disparaging a Kent, the thrust is shrewd enough for Shakespeare not to risk it unless he is confident that Kent's credit with the audience is firm.

This variety and apparent inconsistency give great vitality. From the Kent of the first scene, quick of eye, frank at a question:

> Is not this your son, my lord?

impatient at half answers:

> I cannot conceive you.

yet tolerant, discreetly courteous, dry, self-contained:

> I cannot wish the fault undone, the issue of it being so proper.

but gentle and kindly too:

> I must love you and sue to know you better.

—from this we pass without warning to the impetuous outburst against Lear; and unmannerly though this may be, it is still dignified, collected and cool. From this to the Kent of the borrowed accents—but never more himself than in his disguise, to the man of

> What would'st thou?
> Service.
> Who would'st thou serve?
> You.

Dost thou know me, fellow?

No, sir; but you have that in your countenance which I would fain call master.

What's that?

Authority.

to the Kent of the tripping of Oswald; and, at their next meeting, with Oswald so unwary as to ask him

What dost thou know me for?

to the Kent of

A knave, a rascal, an eater of broken meats; a base, proud, shallow, beggarly, three-suited, hundred-pound, filthy, worsted-stocking knave; a lily-livered, action-taking knave; a whoreson, glass-gazing, super-serviceable, finical rogue; a one-trunk inheriting slave; one that wouldst be a bawd in way of good service, and art nothing but the composition of a knave, beggar, coward, pandar, and the son and heir of a mongrel bitch; one whom I will beat into clamorous whining if thou deniest the least syllable of thy addition.

to the resourceful, humorous disputant of the scene with Cornwall and Regan, and to the philosopher in the stocks, with his

Fortune, good-night; smile once more; turn thy wheel!

Having so opulently endowed him with life, Shakespeare, we may say, can now afford to be thriftier of attention to him for a while; he had better be, we might add, or the balance of the play's interest will go awry. But it is of a piece with the character that, when misfortune overwhelms Lear, Kent should sink himself in it, that his colourfulness should fade, his humour wane, and the rest of the play find him tuned to this

one key of vigilant unquestioning service; till he comes
to the final simplicity of

> I have a journey, sir, shortly to go.
> My master calls me, I must not say no.

Nevertheless Shakespeare does seem in Act IV to lose
interest in him, thus straitened, and he keeps him a place
in the action carelessly enough. Throughout the storm-
scenes, of course, his sober, single-minded concern for
the King does but reinforce his dramatic credit; it is,
besides, a necessary check to their delirium. He could
have even less to say here, and his very presence would
be a strength. It is like Kent not to fuss as poor Gloucester fusses, not to talk when he need not, to think of
the morrow and do the best he can meanwhile. Shakespeare allows him—a just economy—two flashes of emotion; the first when Lear turns to him with

> Wilt break my heart?
> I'd rather break my own . . . .

he says. And once—

> O pity!

No more than that.

It is after he has taken Lear to Dover that, as a character,
he begins to live upon the credit of his past. Shakespeare
seems not quite sure what more he may want of him; he
only does not want him to complicate with his vigorous
personality the crowded later action of the play. What his
purpose may be in sustaining his disguise—

> Pardon, dear madam;
> Yet to be known shortens my made intent:
> My boon I make it that you know me not
> Till time and I think meet.

—is never very clear. But Shakespeare's own purpose here is clear enough; not to spoil Lear's reconciliation with Cordelia, by adding to it a recognition of Kent. The couplet with which Kent ends the scene:

> My point and period will be throughly wrought,
> Or well or ill, as this day's battle's fought.

has in the event neither much significance nor consequence. It is a safe remark and sounds well. We might suppose (we may do so, if we like; but in fact an audience will not stop to consider a commentator's point) that Kent is counting, if Lear is defeated, on serving him still in disguise, when known he could not. But he does not appear in the battle or the defeat; and this we might think (if, again, we stopped to think; but while the play is acting we shall not) as strange as his neglect which had let Lear escape to wander

> As mad as the vex'd sea; singing aloud . . .

But the simple explanation probably is that Shakespeare finds he has no more dramatic use for Kent till he can bring him on, the play all but done, with

> I am come
> To bid my king and master aye good-night.

So he must just keep him in being meanwhile.

That Kent should survive so effectively to the play's end is at once a tribute to the vitality of his first projection and to the tact with which Shakespeare can navigate the shallows of his art. And the actor who can express himself and impress himself upon us as well by silence as by speech will find no difficulties in the part.

THE FOOL

The Fool can never, of course, be to us what he was to the play's first audience. For them, Shakespeare's achievement lay in the double conversion of a stock stage character and a traditional Court figure to transcendent dramatic use. There are few greater pleasures in art than to find the familiar made new; but to us stage Fool and Court Fool alike are strange to start with. Court Fool has, to be sure, a likely claim to a place in the play, and can claim a place too in our historical consciousness. Grant the old King such a favourite: it is good character scheming to contrast his royal caprices with such spaniel affection; dramatic craft at its best to leave Lear in adversity this one fantastic remnant of royalty. This, and much more of intrinsic value, we cannot lose. But what, from the transcended stage Fool, did Shakespeare gain besides?

Elizabethan acting did not inhabit the removed footlight-defended stage of the theatre of today, and all its technique and conventions and the illusion it created differ appropriately in consequence; this is the constant theme of these Prefaces, and must be of any study of the staging of Shakespeare plays. But certain effects, however gained, are common to all drama, certain problems recur. A problem in the writing and acting of tragedy is the alternate creating and relaxing of emotional strain; the tenser the strain, the less long can an audience appreciatively endure it. 'Comic relief' has a crude sound; but, to some degree and in some form or other, the thing it suggests is a necessity. Greek tragedy had 'choric relief'; emotion in the Greek theatre was magnified and rarefied at once, and sharp transitions were neither wanted nor workable. Shakespeare had the constant shift of scene and subject, usual in his theatre, to help him; and his most strenuous scenes, we may remark, tend to be short ones.[25] We may suppose him ever mindful of the difficulty of keeping the attention of a motley audience fixed, but still alert; and in the body of a scene, if it needs must be a long one, we shall always find what may be called 'points of rest and recovery'.

But the problem can be stated in other terms. Tragedy, it may be said, takes us out of ourselves; how else can it be enjoyed? A dash of comedy will, by contrast, restore us to ourselves; yet, for the tragedy's sake, the less conscious of the process we are the better. Here lay for Shakespeare, in this play, the histrionic value of the Fool. He wanted no comic relief in the crude sense; but this familiar stage figure, even though turned to tragic purpose, kept for that audience, if insensibly, its traditional hail-fellow quality. Only the dramatic and human value of the character is preserved us for today to the full. Of the effect of the snatches of song and rhyme, the lyric lightening of the epic strength of these scenes, we keep only the most manifest part. The things themselves are queer to us, and this is just what they should not be. And of the friendly feeling, the sense of being at ease with ourselves, which the stage Fool, a-straddle between play and audience, could create for the Elizabethans, we save nothing at all. We have felt something of the sort as children perhaps, when, at the Pantomime, after the removed mysteries of the transformation scene, came the harlequinade and the clown, cuddling us up to him with his 'Here we are again'. It may seem a far cry from red-hot poker and sausages to *King Lear*. But these indigenous attributes of the Fool are the underlying strength of the part once its acting is in question; and it is Shakespeare's use and restraint and disguise of them at once that is so masterly. Out went the character, as we know, from the eighteenth-century versions of the play; nor actors nor audience, it was thought, could countenance such an aberration. Macready restored it with many misgivings and gave it to a girl to act. The producer today faces another difficulty. He finds a Fool all etherealized by the higher criticism. His first care, in the part's embodying, must be to see restored as much as may be of its lost aboriginal strength. Its actor must sing like a lark, juggle his words so that the mere skill delights us, and tumble around with all the grace in the world. Satisfy these simpler demands, and the subtleties will have their effect; neglect them, and you might as well try to play tunes on a punctured organ stop.

About the Fool's character in the personal sense there is really not much to be said, though it is a subject upon which the romantic commentator has rejoiced to embroider his own fancies. He is, not a half-wit, but—the old word fits—a 'natural'; he does not, that is to say, draw all our practical distinction between sense and nonsense, the wise thing to do, and the unwise. But he lives in a logical world of his own. Lear has petted him as one pets a dog; he shows a dog's fidelity. It is foolish of him, no doubt, to follow his master into such a storm—but, then, he *is* a fool. Shakespeare, having had his dramatic use of him, drops him incontinently; this alone should label the part of merely incidental importance to the scheme of the play. But even this he makes a measure of the human pathos of the creature. We are told by the attendant knight before ever we see him:

> Since my young lady's going into France, sir, the fool hath much pined away.
> No more of that; I have noted it well . . . .

Lear answers (lest we should not note it well enough). But not a word more; above all never a hint from this professional jester himself that he has, or has a right to, any feelings of his own. His jests have grown bitterer lately perhaps, to suit with Lear's changing fortunes; yet, for compensation, he is more full of song than ever. And come weal, come woe, he sticks to his job, sticks to it and to his master till the storm batters him into silence. With a ha'porth of warmth and comfort in him, he flickers bravely into jest again. But his task is done now, and he himself pretty well done for. He tells us so in a very short and bitter jest indeed:

> And I'll go to bed at noon.

And this is the last we hear or see of him; and what happens to him thereafter, who knows or cares? Which is quite according to the jesters'—and players'—code of professional honour, and to the common reward of its observance, as Shakespeare, of all men, would know well. To pursue the Fool beyond the play's bounds, to steep him in extraneous sentiment, is to miss the most characteristically dramatic thing about him.

One minor point about the part is yet an important one. The soliloquy with which Act III, Scene ii, is made to end is certainly spurious.[26] Its own incongruity can be left out of the question; its offence against the dramatic situation disallows it. The very heart of this is Lear's new-found care for the shivering drenched creature at his side.

> Come on, my boy. How dost, my boy? Art cold?...
> Poor fool and knave, I have one part in my heart
> That's sorry yet for thee.

Shakespeare is incapable—so would any other dramatist in his senses be—of stultifying himself by dispatching Lear from the scene immediately after, and letting him leave the Fool behind him.

GLOUCESTER, EDGAR AND EDMUND

Gloucester and his sons are opposite numbers, as the phrase now goes, to Lear and his daughters. Gloucester himself is the play's nearest approach to the average sensual man. The civilized world is full of Gloucesters. In half a dozen short speeches Shakespeare sets him fully before us: turning elderly but probably still handsome; nice of speech if a little pompous; the accomplished courtier (he seems to be Lear's master of ceremonies); vain, as his mock modesty shows, but the joking shamelessness that succeeds it is mainly swagger; an egotist, and blind, knowing least of what he should know most, of his own two sons.

He hath been out nine years, and away he shall again.

That carelessly jovial sentence of banishment for Edmund proves his own death-sentence. Still, who could suspect the modest young newcomer, making his bow with

Sir, I shall study deserving.

of having such unpleasant thoughts in mind?

Gloucester, like so many sensual men, is good nature itself, as long as things go their easy, natural way; but when they fail to he is upset, rattled. Kent's banishment, the quarrel with Cordelia and France, and the King's utter recklessness set his mind off at one tangent and another and make him an easier victim to very simple deceit. We must not, however, appraise either his simplicity or Edgar's, at this moment, with detachment—for by that light, no human being, it would seem, between infancy and dotage, could be so gullible. Shakespeare asks us to allow him the fact of the deception, even as we have allowed him Lear's partition of the kingdom. It is his starting point, the dramatist's 'let's pretend', which is as essential to the beginning of a play as a 'let it be granted' to a proposition of Euclid. And, within bounds, the degree of pretence makes surprisingly little difference. It is what the assumption will commit him to that counts; once a play's action is under way it must develop as logically as Euclid, and far more logically than life. The art of the thing is to reward the spectator for his concession by never presuming on it; one should rather dress up the unlikely in the likelier. Thus Shakespeare makes Gloucester, with his pother about 'these late eclipses of the sun and moon', the sort of man who might at any moment be taken in by any sort of tale; the more improbable, indeed, the better. He makes Edmund plausible even if the incriminating letter is not. And what better way to confirm a nervous, puzzled, opinionated man in an error than to reason calmly with him against it? Your victim will instinctively take the opposite point of view and forget that this was yours to begin with.[27] Does not the credulous nature crave to be deceived? Moreover, Shakespeare's first concern is to develop character, to put us on terms with these people; not till that is done, he knows, will their doings and sufferings really affect us. So it suits him, in any case, to subordinate, for a little, what they do to what they are. And we part from Gloucester in this scene knowing him for a start pretty well.

The sensual man does not stand up very resolutely against blows dealt to his complacent affections. Disillusion leaves Gloucester not only wax in Edmund's hands but more helpless than it belongs to him to be—fair-weather sailor though he has ever been!—in the alien troubles that now centre round him. Shakespeare's manoeuvring of him through these scenes—from the welcome to the 'noble arch and patron' to the moment when his guest's honoured fingers are plucking at his eyes—is a good example of the fruitful economy with which, once a character has 'come alive', its simplest gesture, its very muteness is made significant. And Gloucester has been alive from the beginning; no illustration for a thesis, but unselfconsciously himself. This very unselfconsciousness is turned later to tragic account. Fate's worst revenge on him is that, blinded, he comes to see himself so clearly as he is, and to find the world, which once went so comfortably with him, a moral chaos. We might wonder at the amount of agonized reflection in this kind allotted to him. But mark its culmination:

> The king is mad: how stiff is my vile sense
> That I stand up, and have ingenious feeling
> Of my huge sorrows! Better I were distract:
> So should my thoughts be sever'd from my griefs,
> And woes by wrong imaginations lose
> The knowledge of themselves.

The one thing, it seems, that the average sensual man cannot endure is knowledge of the truth. Better death or madness than that!

Yet which of us must not feelingly protest that the Gloucester, who threads and fumbles his way so well-meaningly about the family battlefield his house is turned into (much against his will), is very harshly used indeed? Is this poetic justice? He does all that one who respects his superiors may do to save Kent from the ignominy of the stocks. He does his best to pacify Lear.

> I would have all well betwixt you.

How familiar is that heartfelt cry of the man who sees no sense in a quarrel! When he does take sides his reasons and his method are not heroic, it is true.

These injuries the king now bears will be revenged home; there is part of a power already footed; we must incline to the king. I will look to him and privily relieve him, go you and maintain talk with the duke, that my charity be not of him perceived. If he asks for me, I am ill and gone to bed.

No, truly, it is not heroic, when battle is joined, to be ill and go to bed. But caution is a sort of a virtue; and the keeping of a family foot in each camp has good sanction. Yet who can be altogether wise? In his next breath comes

If I die for it, as no less is threatened me, the king, my old master, must be relieved.

And this his best impulse is his undoing. Unwittingly he is telling Edmund how best to betray him. He points the way; Edmund has but to follow it—just a little further. Irony deepens when later he calls upon Cornwall to spare him in the sacred name of that hospitality which, towards his king, he himself has so spinelessly betrayed. Yet, 'tied to the stake' he can 'stand the course' courageously enough; and he recovers self-respect in hopeless defiance of his tyrants. With just a little luck he need never have lost it. Now he is blinded and turned helpless from his own doors. Is this poetic justice upon a gentleman, whose worst fault has been to play for safety, his worst blunder to think ill of a man without question and to believe a liar? Disquieting to think that it may be![28]

Edmund is, in wickedness, half-brother to Iago. Having no such great nature as Othello's to work on, Shakespeare has no need of such transcendent villainy; and he lessens and vulgarizes his man by giving him one of those excuses for foul play against the world which a knave likes to find as a point of departure. His first soliloquy is a complete enough disclosure. The fine flourish of

> Thou, Nature, art my goddess....

(finer by its surprise for us in the mouth of the modest young man of the earlier scene), and the magnificent rejection of conventional morality narrow to their objective in

> Well, then,
> Legitimate Edgar, I must have your land.

And from this firm businesslike basis Edmund, except for pure pose, never soars again. The later

> This is the excellent foppery of the world....

is enjoyable argument doubtless, and doubtless he chuckles over it. There is a sporting and imaginative touch, perhaps, in the trick that finally gets rid of Edgar; the stabbing his own arm, we feel, is to his credit. But for the rest, a strict attention to business, and a quick eye to one main chance after the other, suffice him. And this, really, is almost the loathliest thing about the man. He not only betrays his father to Cornwall, but he cants about loyalty the while. He accepts the attentions of Regan and Goneril without surprise or embarrassment (he is a handsome young fellow and he knows it), calculates which will be the more desirable connection, but will leave Goneril to get rid of her husband alone if that risky task has to be undertaken. It even passes through his mind that she herself—if not Regan—may in her turn have to be 'put away'. His tardy repentance does not touch us; and he puts it into practice too tardily.[29] The queer snobbery which prompts him to say to the still visored Edgar

> If thou'rt noble,
> I do forgive thee.

and the still queerer vanity (at such a moment!) of

> Yet Edmund was beloved.
> The one the other poison'd for my sake,
> And after slew herself.

may strike upon some ears as all but ridiculous. He is an ignoble scoundrel and he makes an ignoble end.

Still, his methods have been interesting. The first attack upon his father's credulity was, as we saw, both bold and apt; and what could be safer support to the fiction of Edgar's plot than the counterfeit truth of

> When I dissuaded him from his intent . . .
> he replied,
> Thou unpossessing bastard! dost thou think,
> If I would stand against thee, would the reposal
> Of any trust, virtue, or worth in thee
> Make thy words faith'd? No: what I should deny,—
> As this I would; ay, though thou didst produce
> My very character, I'd turn it all
> To thy suggestion, plot, and damned practice.

For masterly confounding of counsel this should rouse the admiration of the most practised liar. Whether, later, there is need for him to be so snivellingly hypocritical with Cornwall we may question. But he is still on promotion; and that shrewd, forthright brute, if not deceived, will be the more flattered by this tribute of vice to his virtue.

But once he is in the saddle, and when not one royal lady, but two, have lost their heads over him, what a change!

> Know of the duke if his last purpose hold,
> Or whether since he is advised by aught

> To change his course; he's full of alteration
> And self-reproving; bring his constant pleasure.

This he says publicly of no less a man than Albany, whom later he salutes with an ironically patronizing

> Sir, you speak nobly.

He is losing his head, one fears, in the flush of his fire-new fortune. Albany, however, waits his time and prepares for it; this mild gentleman should have been better reckoned with. For, of a sudden, Edmund finds that he has climbed, even as his blinded father set out in misery to climb, to the edge of a steep. And it is an apposite phrase indeed which flashes the depths on him:

> Half-blooded fellow, yes!

—from an Albany not so mild. The wheel is coming circle.

This individual catastrophe and its contriving are a good example of Shakespeare's adapting of end to means (that constant obligation of the dramatist), and of his turning disability to advantage. His very need to compress close these latter incidents of Edmund's rise to fortune helps him make it the more egregious. The fact that but a dozen speeches seem to lift the fellow towards the grasping of the very power of which Lear divested himself at the play's beginning should make our recollection of that modest young man in the background of its first scene the more amazing to us. It is, at this juncture, a breathless business for all concerned. Then at the climax comes the sudden isolation of the upstart, brave in his armour, flushed with his triumph. And Shakespeare releases the tension—and rewards himself for his economy—in the sounding of trumpets, the fine flow and colour of some heroic verse quite in his old style, and all the exciting ceremony of the duel.[30] Late in the play as this comes, and of secondary concern to the greater tragedy as it may be, not a point of its thriftily developed drama must be missed.

Edgar is a 'slow starter' and shows no promise at all as a hero. Not here, however, but in Shakespeare's use of him as Poor Tom will be the actor's greater handicap. For by the time he is free from this arbitrary bondage the play has put our attention and emotions to some strain and we are no longer so well disposed to the development of a fresh serious interest. Otherwise there is every dramatic fitness in his tardy coming to his own. Edmund flashes upon us in pinchbeck brilliance; the worth of Edgar waits discovery, and trial and misfortune must help discover it—to himself above all.

> a brother noble,
> Whose nature is so far from doing harms
> That he suspects none; on whose foolish honesty
> My practices ride easy!

says Edmund of him in proper contempt. 'What are you?' asks his unknowing father, when his fortunes are still at their worst. And he answers:

> A most poor man, made tame to fortune's blows;
> Who, by the art of known and feeling sorrows,
> Am pregnant to good pity.

But, by the play's end, it is to him as well as to Kent that Albany turns with

> Friends of my soul, you twain
> Rule in this realm, and the gor'd state sustain.

What are the steps by which he passes from nobody to somebody?

His very reserve at the beginning can give him a stamp of distinction, and should be made to do so. And the notion of that strange disguise would not come, we may say, to a commonplace man. Through the ravings of Poor Tom we can detect something of the mind of Edgar with its misprision of the sensual life—of his father's life, is it? We can certainly see his pitiful heart; this Shakespeare stresses. But only in the soliloquies that end Act III, Scene vi, and begin Act IV do we discover the full mind of the man[31]:

> When we our betters see bearing our woes,
> We scarcely think our miseries our foes.
> Who alone suffers, suffers most i' the mind,
> Leaving free things and happy shows behind;
> But then the mind much sufferance doth o'erskip,
> When grief hath mates, and bearing fellowship. . . .

and

> Yet better thus, and known to be contemn'd,
> Than still contemn'd and flatter'd. To be worst,
> The lowest and most dejected thing of fortune,
> Stands still in esperance, lives not in fear;
> The lamentable change is from the best;
> The worst returns to laughter. . . .

We seem to have found the play's philosopher. And the sententiousness of the earlier soliloquy, differing both in form and tone from anything that has preceded it in the play, is surely a deliberate contrivance to lower the tension of the action and to prepare us for the calmer atmosphere—by comparison—of the play's ending. Shakespeare may afterwards have repented of it as sounding too sententious and as coming uselessly for its wider

purpose immediately before the blinding of Gloucester.
But Edgar's philosophy of indifference to fortune, of
patience with life itself, of the good comfort of fellowship,
is now, certainly, to dominate the play. It is summed up
for us more than once.

> Bear free and patient thoughts.

he tells his father, when, by his queer stratagem—again,
it was not the notion of a commonplace mind—he has
saved him from despair. His playing the peasant with
the insufferable Oswald is, yet again, not commonplace;
and, having killed him:

> He is dead. I am only sorry
> He had no other deathsman.[32]

To him is given the answer to Gloucester's deadly

> As flies to wanton boys, are we to the gods;
> They kill us for their sport.

in

> therefore, thou happy father,
> Think that the clearest gods, who make them honours
> Of men's impossibilities, have preserved thee.

To him is given

> The gods are just, and of our pleasant vices
> Make instruments to plague us.

But before this, his good name and his father's death
justly avenged, what is the first thing he says as he
discloses himself to the doubly damned scoundrel lying
at his feet?

> Let's exchange charity.

Edgar, in fact, has become a man of character indeed, modest, of a discerning mind, and, in this pagan play, a very Christian gentleman.[33]

BURGUNDY, FRANCE, ALBANY, CORNWALL

Burgundy and France hardly outpass convention, though the one gains enough character from his laconic indifference, while the spirit and quality of France's speeches should keep him a pleasant memory to the play's end.[34]

Cornwall has 'character' in abundance. He and Albany stand all but mute at their first appearance.[35] But from our next sight of him to our last he justifies in action and speech Gloucester's description:

> My dear lord,
> You know the fiery quality of the duke;
> How unremoveable and fix'd he is
> To his own course.

He is a man, we may suppose, in the prime of life; old enough, at least, to say to Edmund

> thou shalt find a dearer father in my love.

He is by no means a stupid man: the cynical humour with which he appraises Kent shows that. He asserts himself against his wife as Albany does not. He can speak up to Lear when need be, but he is not too swift to do it. In his vindictiveness he still keeps his head.

> Go seek the traitor Gloucester,
> Pinion him like a thief, bring him before us.
> Though well we may not pass upon his life
> Without the form of justice, yet our power

> Shall do a courtesy to our wrath, which men
> May blame but not control.

But this hardly makes him the more likable. And though we might allow him some credit for at least doing his own dirty work, it is evident that he enjoys Gloucester's blinding, for he sets about it with a savage jest. The taste of blood seems to let loose all the wild beast in him; and, like a wild beast, Shakespeare has him dispatched. Yet Cornwall is a forceful character; and there are those who—having no more concern with them than to profit by their forcefulness—can find, strangely enough, something to admire in such men. So he may be allowed a certain dog-toothed attractiveness in performance.

Albany is at the opposite pole. He prefers a quiet life with Goneril while he can contrive to lead it, even at the cost of some self-respect.

> Striving to better, oft we mar what's well.

seems to stand as his motto; and it sounds the more sententious by its setting in a rhymed couplet. His 'milky gentleness', his 'harmful mildness' ring true enough as accusations: does he think to tame a tigress with a platitude? His wife, quite naturally, departs to seek Regan's help without him.

Much has happened, though, by the time we see him again, when Goneril is on the full tide of reckless triumphant wickedness. She takes no heed of Oswald's

> never man so changed . . .

still presumes on

> the cowish terror of his spirit . . .

and even, when she meets him changed indeed, is blind
and deaf to the change. That Albany had loved his wife
is made plain. We hear him speak in his quiet way of
'the great love' he bore her. He has been slow to think
ill of her. But he is of those who let their wrath gather
beneath a placid surface till, on a sudden, it boils over,
and if the cause of it lies deep they are never the same
again. Shakespeare, who cannot spare much space for his
development, gives us this impression of the man by
allowing us chiefly these contrasted sights of him, the long
interval between. And the first stern clash with Goneril
has a double purpose and nets a double dramatic gain.
It wins Albany the authoritative standing that he now
needs in the play, and it shows us a Goneril so possessed
by self-will that our own surprise at the change in him
turns to surprise that she can be so oblivious of it. We
may count her a doomed creature from this moment.

Henceforth he is pitted against Edmund; the aristocrat
against the upstart; the man with nothing to gain for
himself against the man who must win and still win or
perish; the man who, to the taunt of 'moral fool', can
answer

> Where I could not be honest,
> I never yet was valiant.

against the man who can tell his follower as he sends
him to commit an atrocious murder:

> know thou this, that men
> Are as the time is; to be tender-minded
> Does not become a sword; thy great employment
> Will not bear question; either say thou'lt do 't,
> Or thrive by other means.

The world's allegiance is ever swaying between such
leaderships.

Albany, once in action, is as distinguished a figure as any in the play. Shakespeare endows him with a fine sense of irony. The slight sting in the tail of his compliment to Edmund after the battle:

> Sir, you have showed to-day your valiant strain,
> And fortune led you well. . . .

the cutting courtesy of

> Sir, by your patience,
> I hold you but a subject of this war,
> Not as a brother.

his cool preparation of his stroke; the stroke itself:

> Stay yet, hear reason. Edmund, I arrest thee
> On capital treason; and, in thy arrest,
> This gilded serpent. For your claim, fair sister,
> I bar it in the interest of my wife;
> 'Tis she is sub-contracted to this lord,
> And I, her husband, contradict your banns.
> If you will marry, make your loves to me,
> My lady is bespoke.

—are not bad for a moral fool.

Nor does he trust to the appearance of the unknown champion for Edmund's undoing. He throws his own gauntlet down. A touch of gallantry, though Shakespeare does not—does not need to—compromise his dignity by setting him to fight. And he is left from now to the play's end in command of its action.[36]

OSWALD AND THE MINOR PARTS

A modern audience must lose almost as much of the flavour of Oswald as of the Fool; and more still must be lost if he is stripped of his doublet and hose, forbidden his swagger and his curtseys and thrust back into the dark ages. We cannot be expected to cheer—as I doubt not Shakespeare's audience did—when Kent breaks out with

> That such a slave as this should wear a sword,
> Who wears no honesty!

nor to take the precise point of Lear's

> How now, where's that mongrel?

that newfangled fellow, neither gentleman nor plain servant, mimicking the manners of the one, doing dirtier work than the other. Kent sizes him up when he dresses him down, with enjoyable completeness; so does Lear, later, in a dozen words:

> This is a slave, whose easy-borrowed pride
> Dwells in the fickle grace of her he follows.

So does Edgar, having rid the world of him, as

> a serviceable villain;
> As duteous to the vices of thy mistress
> As badness would desire.

Oswalds have existed in every age and been good game for abuse, but the London of Shakespeare's day had evidently produced an unusually fine crop of them. His own sayings are colourless compared with what is said of him. It follows, then, that his 'Ay, madams' and 'No, madams', his 'I'll not be strucken, my lord,' his 'Prithee, if thou lovest me, tell me,' and his 'Out, dunghill', when the peasant's cudgel threatens to knock his dishonourable sword out of his hand, must answer exactly in accent and attitude, as he himself in look and manner, to the very sort of being Shakespeare had in mind. In himself he is nothing; a 'whoreson zed', an 'unnecessary letter', and he should seem no more. But, as a tailor made him, he must be tailored right.

It remains to notice one or two of Shakespeare's minuter touches. When Gloucester has been blinded, branded a traitor and turned from his own house to smell his way to Dover, he finds one fearless friend; the old peasant who has been his tenant and his father's tenant 'these fourscore years'. The savagery of the blinding itself had stirred one common fellow to risk and lose his life stopping the worst of it. Two other common fellows have the charity to bind up the wounds; but they'll risk no more than that. The old peasant, too old himself to go far with his lord, shakes a sad head at leaving him in such company as Poor Tom, and will risk his fortunes to do Gloucester, in his ruin and disgrace, a last simple service. Close following the transcendent scenes of Lear's madness and the extreme brutality of the blinding comes this interlude of servant and peasant, of common humanity in its bravery and charity with its simple stumbling talk. The whole effect is made in a dozen lines or so, but gains importance by its homespun contrast and by its placing across the main dividing line of the play's action.

And for a happy instance of Shakespeare's power to suggest a man in a dozen words, take the reply of the Captain to whom Edmund confides the murder of Lear and Cordelia:

> I cannot draw a cart nor eat dried oats;
> If it be man's work, I'll do it.

Staging and Costume

No more need be urged, I hope, against a realistic staging of the play or anything approaching one. But

whether the single alternative to this is the actuality of
Shakespeare's own theatre is another question, which the
producer must answer for himself. If he protests that his
audience will never sit so unconsciously before a reproduction of the Globe stage as did Shakespeare's before
the thing itself one cannot contradict him. But he cuts
from the anchorage at his peril. And the doubt is as to
whether when he has found some, presumably, atmos-
pheric sort of background, which does not positively
conflict with the play's stagecraft, the result—for all its
visual beauty—will be worth the risk and the trouble.

Abide by Shakespeare's own stage, and no questions
of importance arise upon the use of it. But for Edgar's
moment 'above', some need for the masking of Lear's
'state', and again for the discovery of the joint-stools and
bench in the scene of the mock trial, the play could
indeed be acted upon a barer stage than was the
Globe's.[37] The great chair with the unconscious Lear in
it may be more conveniently carried from an inner stage,
and Poor Tom will emerge more effectively from one
than from a side-door. But this is all; and it may even
be that Shakespeare minimized such localization as his
theatre did afford him to give the play spaciousness of
action, and to magnify his characters the more in iso-
lating them from needless detail of circumstance. Let the
producer, at any rate—and at all costs—provide for the
action's swift unencumbered movement and for our concentration upon the characters themselves, in whom
everything is concentrated.

As for costume, this is one of the few plays in which
Shakespeare took some trouble to do more than its
subject itself would do to dissociate it from his own time;
though even so he will not have relied overmuch upon
costume to help him. But only here and there is his own
seventeenth-century patent, and that in character or

incident of minor importance. The prevailing atmosphere and accent is barbaric and remote. Edmund's relationship to Iago may seem to us to give him a certain Italianate flavour, and Edgar's beginning suggests bookishness and the Renaissance. But clothe these two as we please, their substance will defy disguise. Oswald, as we have argued, is a topical picture; in the Ancient Briton he will be all but obliterated. That must be faced. Of the Fool, by shifting him back a dozen centuries, we lose little, because, as we have argued, we are bound already to lose so much. And if a Fool in a barbarous king's retinue seems to us an anachronism (though it may be doubted if—for all the preciseness that would take offence at a Henry V in doublet and hose—it will), the fantasy of the part marks it out as the fittest note of relief from consistency. To consistency in such matters no dated play of Shakespeare can be submitted. Here our main losses by desertion of seventeenth-century habit and manners will end. And such anachronism as may lie in Cordelia's chance of being Duchess of Burgundy, in 'base foot-ball player' and 'unfee'd lawyer', in the stocks, in some of Poor Tom's talk and Lear's ravings, and in the procedure of the challenge and the duel, will be inconsiderable however the characters are clothed.

So a producer is free to balance these items against an imagined Britain, whose king swears

> by the mysteries of Hecate and the night . . .

(not to mention Apollo), and where a Duke of Cornwall turns public executioner. There is no doubt, I think, in which scale advantage lies. The play should be costumed according to the temper that Shakespeare has given it, a splendid barbaric temper. It is equally clear that archaeological accuracy profits nothing. Nor should the

producer lose more than he need of such sophistication
as Shakespeare himself retained.

The Music

ABOUT the music there is little to be said. I do not
imagine much improvement possible upon 'the consort
of viols', to the quiet harmonies of which Lear was
meant, one presumes, to be waked. The sennet that
announces his first regal appearance should be noted, as
well as the flourish to herald France and Burgundy, and
the ceremonial difference between the two. The *Horns
within*, which prelude Lear's return from hunting, ask no
comment. A trumpet is used with dramatic effect before
Cornwall's entrance in Act II, Scene i; it reinforces
Gloucester's excitement. The same sound stirs Lear a
little later and strings him up for the encounter with
Goneril. And, towards the play's end, the triple sounding
by the herald, to be answered, when our suspense is
keenest, by Edgar's trumpet without, is a most carefully
calculated dramatic effect.[38] We have noticed earlier how
the battle in which Cordelia's forces are defeated is
dramatically minimized; its musical symbolism consists
only of an alarum and an alarum and retreat. But the
Drum afar off, to the ominous sound of which the longest
and most varied scene of the fourth act closes, has very
definite value. So has the dead march with which the
play itself ends.

The Fool is allotted no formal and completed song,
but, needless to say, his snatches of melody should be
melodious indeed. This musical and lyrical relief to the
strain of Lear's passion is, as we have argued elsewhere,
an essential part of the play's stagecraft. The technique
of the singing should not be artificial; rather that of an
accomplished folk-song singer. And where no authentically

traditional tunes exist, folk music will prove a sufficient quarry.

The Text

THE complications of the text are troublesome. Corruptions, obvious and suspected, apart, the producer is confronted by the problem of the three hundred lines, or nearly, that the Quartos give and the Folio omits, and of the hundred given by the Folio and omitted from the Quartos. Editors, considering only, it would seem, that the more Shakespeare we get the better, bring practically the whole lot into the play we read. But a producer must ask himself whether these two versions do not come from different prompt books, and whether the Folio does not, both in cuts and additions, sometimes represent Shakespeare's own second thoughts. In general, surely, the Folio is of better authority; it is at least more carefully transcribed. Some of its cuts are of passages which seem to have been found constructionally unnecessary. Some only 'ease' the dialogue; they are of varying importance and aptness. Where Quarto and Folio offer alternatives, to adopt both versions may make for redundancy or confusion.[39]

To deal with the major differences. In the scene of the dividing of the kingdom the Folio's stressed identification of Albany and Cornwall, France and Burgundy, seems deliberate and is certainly valuable. Of the additions to the Gloucester-Edmund-Edgar scene the same may be said. Gloucester can hardly be shown too distracted, and the hiding-away of Edgar from his father is a good point made. But, in compensation, the Folio cuts the mockery of Gloucester's foibles with which Edmund preludes his attempt on Edgar's confidence—and one sees why.

In Goneril's first scene with Oswald the Folio's omissions save some repetition and show her to us terser and less familiar with her servant. A Folio cut in the Fool's part a little later—his rhyming upon the 'sweet and bitter fool', and the joke about monopolizing—may seem at a first glance a little clumsy. But we shall hardly appreciate the gibe at monopolies unless we rewrite it 'trusts'; probably the Quarto's audiences had appreciated it too well. The whole cut is a useful tightening of the dialogue. Yet a little later the Folio gives us (as the Quarto does not) a passage in which Goneril justifies herself to Albany; undoubtedly useful.

When Lear finds Kent in the stocks and has listened in silence to the story of his being set there, by the Quarto

O, how this mother swells up toward my heart. . . .

follows immediately upon Kent's story. The Folio gives the Fool a little piping song, while Lear still stands speechless, his agony upon him. The dramatic effect will be appreciably different.

Later the Folio alone gives us a passage in which Regan justifies Goneril.

In Act III, Scene i, the Folio cuts some important lines out of the Gentleman's second speech. In particular

Strives in his little world of man to outscorn
The to-and-fro-conflicting wind and rain.

has vanished. An inefficient actor might have been the cause of this. A few lines later Folio and Quarto offer us alternative cuts. That of the Folio is perhaps the clumsier of the two. It stresses the call for Cordelia's help but barely hints at her army's landing, which the Quarto emphasizes. We may or may not have here the cutting of a common original (of which still more may have existed; for of the

> servants, who seem no less,
> Which are to France the spies and speculations
> Intelligent of our state...

we do not hear again). The object of the cut in both cases—and possibly the cutting of the Gentleman's speech also—is evidently to shorten this prelude to Lear's great entrance. What should a producer do here? Shakespeare leaves us to the end a little unconvinced by the machinery of Cordelia's return. There is no dramatic profit in the confusion. Neither text may be as Shakespeare left it. But in this instance I prefer the Quarto's to an amalgam of the two.

Of Merlin's prophecy I have spoken elsewhere.[40]

Let us in passing note the Folio's most important addition of two lines' preparation for the critical

> Poor naked wretches, wheresoe'er you are...

In them the kindness to the half-drowned Fool is emphasized; and he is (I think) sent off the stage so that there may be no danger whatever of discord or incongruity. The actor of the Fool, possibly, was never quite to be relied on; and even if he could be, there was always the chance that some buffoon in the audience would vent an incongruous guffaw at the mere sight of him sitting there. But, above all, by these two lines the meaning and intention of what is to come are emphasized:

> In, boy; go first. You houseless poverty—
> Nay, get thee in. *I'll pray, and then I'll sleep.*

I italicize the vitally important phrase. It is dangerous to dogmatize; but this addition has to me all the air of being a second thought of Shakespeare's own.

We come to the Folio's omission of the mock trial. Time may, as we said, have demanded some omissions, and this scene may have been chosen rather than something better liked by the actors or (seemingly) audience. It can hardly have proved ineffective, technically 'daring' though it is. It certainly does not today; and very certainly one cannot imagine Shakespeare regretting he had written it.

The cut at the end of this scene, however, asks more consideration; for a purely dramatic reason can be found for the omission of Edgar's soliloquy. It must lower the tension of the action. This may damage the scene of Gloucester's blinding, which follows immediately; and if an act-pause is to follow, the tension will, of course, be lowered then. The chief purpose of the soliloquy, moreover, is to give Edgar a fresh start in his dramatic career. It is a quiet start, the effect of which the violent scene that follows must do much to obliterate. When the Folio, then, postpones it to the beginning of Act IV, it does Edgar a double service, as the Quarto doubles the disservice by making the second soliloquy, when it comes, seem dramatically redundant. Without hesitation, I should here follow the Folio text. The further cutting of Kent's lines, however,

> Oppressed nature sleeps . . .

is probably due to a quick closing of the inner stage, which may have obviated the lifting of the sleeping Lear, and it has not the same validity.

The Folio also cuts the significant piece of dialogue between the two servants with which the third act ends. I cannot pretend to say why, if it was not that when this text was settled, the actors to speak the lines were lacking. No one need abide by this cut.

The disappearance of Edgar's 'Obidicut, Hobbididance' and the rest from the first scene with his father is, I think, to the good. A few lines before he says:

I cannot daub it further.

And in any case the effect of the mad lingo will have been exhausted in the scenes with Lear.

We next come to some ruthless cutting of Albany by the Folio. Shakespeare may have yielded here to the exigencies of bad acting or to a wish to knit the action more closely. But he is taking some pains at this juncture to develop Albany, and we shall be on the safe side in keeping to the fuller text.

Now, however, the Folio omits one entire scene. It is a carpentered scene if ever there was one. It begins with a lame explanation of the nonappearance of the King of France; it goes on to a preparation for the reappearance of Cordelia and it ends with some unconvincing talk about Lear's 'burning shame' and Kent's disguise. I could better believe that Shakespeare cut it than wrote it. There is, certainly, a little life in the description of Cordelia, and a case can be made for so heralding her return to the play. The rest is explanation of what is better left unexplained; and whoever, between the making of the Quarto and the Folio, discovered this—Shakespeare or another—did the play a good service, which we shall wisely profit by.

The remaining differences between the two versions show, in the Folio, a further cutting of explanatory stuff, by which we may well abide; a certain slicing into Albany and Edmund that neither hurts them much now, nor, it is true, does much to spur the action; the loss of one or two lines (Cordelia's in particular) that we shall not want to lose, and the gain of a few that seem good second thoughts. There are, besides, one or two changes that seem merely to reflect change in stage practice as between Quarto and Folio.

On the whole, then—and if he show a courageous discretion—I recommend a producer to found himself on the Folio. For that it does show some at least of Shakespeare's own reshapings I feel sure.

Among other slightly vexed questions, the following are particularly worth attention (the lineal references are to the [English] Arden Shakespeare).

Act I, Scene i, 35. There is no authority for Edmund's exit, and the producer is quite at liberty to let him stay and listen to the momentous proceedings.

Scene v, 1. I give a guess that 'Gloucester' in this line is a slip for 'Cornwall'. There is no other evidence that Lear writes to the Earl of Gloucester, nor any reason he should nor any evidence at all that Cornwall lived near the town.

52-3. This couplet has the sanction (as Merlin's prophecy has not) of both Quarto and Folio. But I find its authenticity hard to credit. Shakespeare could write bawdry, and sometimes at what seem to us the unlikeliest moments. This does not smack of the Fool, though, or of what Shakespeare wants of him.

Act II, Scene i, 20. *Enter Edgar.* This stage direction is wrongly placed—and typically—in modern editions. The Quarto places it four lines, the Folio a line, earlier. Even the Folio, then, shows that he enters on the upper stage and is visible to the audience before Edmund sees him. It may seem a small matter, but the difference between an independent entrance and being called on like a dog is appreciable, and can affect a character's importance. Edgar does descend, of course.

Scene ii, 168-73. 'Nothing almost sees miracles, But misery . . . and shall find time From this enormous state, seeking to give Losses their remedies.' Cut this much, and an actor can make sense of a passage otherwise as obscure as it is evidently corrupt.

Scene iii. I think, on the whole, that there is no scene-division here; there is not, that is to say, a cleared stage. Curtains might be drawn before Kent in the stocks, but he may as well sit there asleep while Edgar soliloquizes. On an *unlocalized* stage I doubt its puzzling even a modern audience if he does; it certainly would not have troubled Shakespeare's.

Act III, Scene iii. The Quarto stage-direction *Enter ... with lights* shows, I think, if nothing else does, the use of the inner stage for this scene.

Scene vii, 23. Neither Quarto nor Folio specifies Oswald's exit, and they get Edmund's and Goneril's wrong. But it is plain that Oswald should be gone immediately on the command to get horses for his mistress. Edmund's and Goneril's leavetaking then stands out the plainer, and the 'strange œilliads and most speaking looks' that pass between them as they go may be made noticeable to Regan—and to us.

Act IV, Scene iv, 6. 'Centurie' says the Quarto and 'centery' the Folio; and this surely will be understood even now (and whatever the anachronism) to mean a hundred men. Why send one sentry to look for Lear? And why a sentry, anyhow?

Act V, Scene iii, 161. 'Ask me not what I know.' The Quarto gives this to Goneril and marks her exit accordingly. It is at least a question whether the Folio's change is not erroneous. For Edmund's so sudden change of front is not easily explicable.

284. This is the first and only indication that Kent's name in disguise has been 'Caius'. I cannot dis-

cover that any editor has commented upon the strangeness of Kent—Kent of all people, and at this moment of all others—asking Lear, apparently, a kind of conundrum. The Pied Bull Quarto at least gives no note of interrogation. If the line can be spoken as if it meant

Your servant Kent, who was your servant Caius...

it will at least not be confusing. Can it not, perhaps, be so read? Kent in his next line plainly appropriates the question to himself.

324. The Quarto gives the last speech to Albany, the Folio to Edgar. Convention would allot it to Albany as the man of rank. 'We that are young' sounds more like Edgar. But remembering how much Albany's part is cut in the Folio, it is likely, I think, that this change to Edgar was deliberately made, and therefore it should stand.

1927; PARTLY REVISED IN 1935

Notes

1 Elliston and Kean, after a little hesitation, went so far as to restore the tragic ending. Then, in 1838, Macready acted Shakespeare's play again. But even he tampered with its structure, and—by much omission—with its text.

2 Whom Shakespeare carefully keeps out of the angry scenes which lead to Lear's self-banishment to the wild and the storm.

3 Bradley argues in a footnote that *because* Shakespeare's 'means of imitating a storm were so greatly inferior to ours' he could not have 'had the stage-performance only or chiefly in view in composing these scenes'. But this is, surely, to view Shakespeare's theatre and its craft with modern eyes. The contemporary critic would have found it easier to agree that just

119

because your imitation storm was such a poor affair you must somehow make your stage effect *without* relying on it.

4 Modern scenic productions, even at their simplest, not only destroy this unity of impression, but lengthen the performance of the plays considerably, and the acting habits they have engendered lengthen them still more. Mr Nugent Monck has produced *King Lear* at the Maddermarket Theatre, Norwich, upon an unlocalized stage. He cut approximately 750 of the 3340 lines of text (the Folio will give authority for the cutting of some 200), allowed a ten minutes' interval, did not play overrapidly, and the whole performance only lasted two hours and a half.

5 Therefore the producer who will for the sake of his scenery (as has been the pleasant picture-stage custom) run two or three of the storm-scenes into one, presents himself and his Lear with failure.

6 We find, too, at this point, some signs that the emphasis of the play's whole scheme was altered.

> Have you heard of no likely wars toward,
> 'Twixt the Dukes of Cornwall and Albany?

Curan asks Edmund, who answers 'Not a word'. Edmund, with admirable promptitude, turns the notion to the further confusing of the so easily confused Edgar, but the wars themselves come to nothing. Kent, in an involved speech in Act III (for him most uncharacteristically involved), suggests that it is the threat of them which is bringing the French army to England. But the vagueness is suspicious. It looks a little as if Shakespeare had thought of making the hypocrite inheritors of Cordelia's portion fall out over it (an obvious nemesis) and had changed his mind. There are slight signs indeed that greed of possessions was to have been the axis for the whole play to turn upon. It begins with the parting of the realm; and

> Legitimate Edgar, I must have your land. . . .

is the coping point of Edmund's first soliloquy. Did the discovery of deeper spiritual issues in Lear's own character and fate give us the present play? Another and a later change in the plot can be divined. The King of France comes armed with Cordelia to Lear's rescue, as is natural. Then, by virtue of the clumsiest few lines in the play, he is sent back again. Did Shakespeare originally mean Cordelia to restore her father to his throne as in the old play; but would a French victory in England not have done? It may be; though I cannot think he ever intended Lear to survive. On the other hand, Cordelia herself is not a figure predoomed to death. This catastrophe, though the moral violence of the play may aesthetically justify it, and though it is needed dramatically, as a final blow to Lear (see p. 75 for the fuller argument of this), always seems to me a wrench from his first plan. This decided on, though, he would certainly have to get rid of France. The point for the producer is that the Folio cuts the clumsy explanation, as if on the principle—and it is an excellent one in the theatre—of: 'Never explain, never apologize.' In fact it cuts the whole scene, which later contains as dramatically feeble an excuse for the delay in handing Lear over to his daughter's care, though it gives none for the devoted Kent letting the distracted old man out of his sight to roam the fields crowned with wild flowers. I think on the whole that the Folio gives a producer a good lead. Yet another slight change of plan may be guessed at; it would effect some economy in the working-out of the subplot. Edmund says to Gloucester about Edgar

> If your honour judge it meet, I will place you where you shall hear us confer of this . . . and that without any further delay than this very evening.

But he never does. Shakespeare may have remembered, besides, that he had lately used this none too fresh device in *Othello*.

7 It is worth remarking here upon the fact that of Edgar's two soliloquies—the one which ends Act III, Scene vi, and the one which begins Act IV—the Folio omits the first. They are somewhat redundant in mood if not in matter. The interesting thing is that the Folio omission is of a speech ending a

scene and moralizing upon the event; it forms a 'considering point'. Without it the catastrophe to Gloucester is linked more closely to Lear's misfortunes, and the long due development of Edgar's character then begins—and importantly—the fourth act. For further argument upon this point, see pp. 100, 114.

8 The meeting of mad Lear and blind Gloucester (I give the scene more attention on p. 70) is, of course, most germane to the play's idea—a more important thing to Shakespeare than the mere story—but it does check the march of the story.

9 And this must not be counted as chance, for the bodies of Goneril and Regan have been brought on—why else?

10 It is, moreover, an old device with Shakespeare. Set beside Lear's

> O! reason not the need . . .

Juliet's

> Hath Romeo slain himself? Say thou but 'I'
> And that bare vowel 'I' shall poison more
> Than the death-dealing eye of cockatrice.
> I am not I, if there be such an 'I',
> Or those eyes shut that make thee answer 'I'.
> If he be slain say 'I' or if not, no;
> Brief sounds determine of my weal or woe.

The puns may destroy its emotional value for us, though they did not for the Elizabethans. But the effect aimed at is about the same. The difference in the means to it may be made one measure of Shakespeare's development of his art. Not but that he could pun dramatically to the end. He came, however, to prefer single shots to fusillades.

11 The 'Away, away', is thus spoken to the propitiatory Albany, and has no reference to the servants, who have already been sent off, nor, I think, to Lear's own departure. The point is disputable, no doubt, and I would not go to the stake for my reading of it. The Quartos have 'Go, go, my people' repeated, as if his first order had not been obeyed. I must leave it to better judges of their origin and value to say whether this is

mere muddlement of text. But, even if it is not, the Folio's change of phrase might cover a change of meaning too.

12 But the outward signs of exhaustion must begin to be upon him.

13 There are practical reasons for postponing the entering of the hovel by a scene. For Kent to lead Lear elsewhere fits both with the agitated movement of the action and the freedom of Elizabethan stage method. It enables Shakespeare both to relieve the high tension of the storm-scenes and to provide for the continuity of the Gloucester-Edmund story. And he takes advantage of all this to show us some further battering at Lear's sanity. Note in particular the ominously broken thoughts and sentences of the end of the speech to Kent just before the hovel is reached; and these, as ominously, are set between connected, reasoned passages.

14 It is worth noting that the Folio cuts out the lunatic trial of Regan and Goneril. This episode proves so admirable on the stage that it is hard to suppose Shakespeare's actor failed to make it effective. But if it was a question of time and a choice between two scenes, doubtless his audience would be supposed to prefer the rhetoric of the storm.

15 And Kent is unknown to Lear and Edgar to his father, as we shall sufficiently remember.

16 In the Quarto another preceding scene is also concerned with him.

17 *Mad*, says the stage direction, and no more; the usual *fantastically dressed with wild flowers* is Capel's addition. But something of the sort is justified by Cordelia's speech in the earlier scene. And the dramatic purpose of them is plain: to emphasize the contrast between this and our last sight of him amid the barren wildness of the heath and the storm.

There are signs, it may be noted, that this Gloucester-Lear encounter is a second thought on Shakespeare's part. Apart from its redundance to the action, the Gloucester-Edgar scene is complete without it; and originally, one would guess, Gloucester's

Henceforth I'll bear
Affliction till it do cry out itself
'Enough, enough! and die.

was followed directly by Edgar's

Well pray you, father!

18 The (superficial) inappositeness of this passage is quoted no-
    wadays as evidence of Shakespeare's morbid occupation,
    about now, with the uncleaner aspects of sex. But it is by no
    means inapposite to the larger moral scheme of the play.
    Goneril's lust has become an important factor in the action.
    Shakespeare cannot give much space to its developments, nor
    does he care to set the boys acting women to deal directly
    and elaborately with such matters. So he uses, I think, this
    queer intuition of the mad mind as a mirror in which the
    vileness is reflected and dilated.

19 Shakespeare kept—and transformed—this piece of business
    from the old play; for Cordelia kneels, too, of course. It
    should be given its full value.

20 That scene in the old play haunted Shakespeare.

21 Bradley has an admirable note upon this passage, just such a
    fine piece of perception as we expect from him. Lear, he says,
    at the very last, thinks that Cordelia lives, and dies of the joy
    of it.

22 And certain small alterations from Quarto to Folio emphasize
    this.

23 Act IV, Scene iii.

24 If it be said that there is nothing in the Kent of Act IV which,
    upon analysis, belies his character, yet this Preface is concerned
    also with his presentment, and that is ineffective and even
    halting. But what of his sudden outburst in Act IV, Sc. iii:

It is the stars;
    The stars above us, govern our conditions. . . .

—is this the authentic Kent? And even if Shakespeare were
here starting to develop a new phase of the man, he never
goes on.

For a masterly analysis of the whole character we should
turn to A. C. Bradley's lecture on *King Lear*.

25 This play apart, they are noticeably so in *Macbeth* and in
    Antony and Cleopatra. In *Hamlet* and in *Othello* it may be said

they are not. But in *Hamlet* the action is—and characteristically—not consistently strenuous; and the sustaining of the anguish in *Othello* is typical of the tragedy, helps give us the heroic measure of Othello himself.

26 And surely it is time that all editions of Shakespeare put certain passages, whose fraud can be agreed upon, in expurgatorial brackets. We are ready for another—and another sort of—Bowdler.

27 But it follows that upon these lines we cannot be brought to a very close knowledge of Edgar too. Give him the same scope, and he must either get on the track of the truth or prove himself as great a fool as his father. So Shakespeare, now and at his next appearance, does as little with him as possible. This delays—and dangerously—our gaining interest in him. But a play survives sins of omission when the smallest sin of commission may damn it. Besides, time is valuable; and a subplot cannot, for the moment, be spared much more. The likelihood of the detail of this traffic between father and sons, the sending of letters, the 'retire with me to my lodging . . . there's my key' and the rest, depends somewhat upon the large, loose organization of a great nobleman's household of that day, of which Shakespeare's audience would know well enough.

28 For an earlier stroke of irony—only to be fully appreciated perhaps by the shade of Lady Gloucester—consider the exclamation wrung from the distracted old man at the climax of his wrath against Edgar

> O strong and fasten'd villain!
> Would he deny his letter? *I never got him.*

And this to Edmund his bastard!

29 His 'Ask me not what I know', in which he takes example from Goneril—and Iago—is given by one Quarto and some editors to Goneril herself, with (I fancy) good enough reason.

30 Compare the 'defiances' of this scene with the passage between Mowbray and Norfolk in the beginning of *Richard II*.

31 The Folio rejects the first of those two and (see note 7) the producer may be wise to.

32 'Chill pick your teeth, sir', suggests that he stabs him, either with a knife he wears, or, possibly, with Oswald's own dagger, wrested after a tussle.

33 He is, I think, as true a gentleman as the plays give us. And he is kept himself and no mere moralizer to the last. When Lear sinks dying, it is Edgar who starts forward to recover him, till Kent checks him with the immortal

> Vex not his ghost: O! let him pass; he hates him
> That would upon the rack of this tough world
> Stretch him out longer.

For Edgar is still very young.

34 Here is one of the difficulties incidental to the production of such a play as *King Lear* with a company gathered in for the occasion. The quality of the actors available tends to diminish with the importance of the parts. Pay apart, an actor of authority and distinction will not attach himself to a theatre for the sole purpose of playing France. Hence the need of an established company with all its compensating opportunities. France is a powerful king and Cordelia's husband; and if he does not impress us as he should, and lodge himself in our memories, not only is the play immediately the poorer, but Cordelia, returning, is robbed of a background of great importance to her.

35 By the text of the Quarto absolutely mute.

36 Though the last speech should possibly, in accordance with the Folio, be Edgar's.

37 There are one or two signs that the stage to which the Folio version was fitted differed a little from that of the Quarto.

38 Beethoven found a similar one useful in *Fidelio*.

39 I speak from now on of 'the Quarto' because for the purposes of this argument the 'Pied Bull' and 'Butter' Quartos might be one.

40 P. 91.

Notes

Notes

Notes

Notes

Notes

Notes

Notes

Notes

Notes